Voices of the Oral Deaf

Voices of the Oral Deaf

Fourteen Role Models Speak Out

JIM REISLER

McFarland & Company, Inc., Publishers

Jefferson, North Carolina, and London

The author's royalties from the sale of this book will be donated to the League for the Hard of Hearing.

Library of Congress Cataloguing-in-Publication Data

Reisler, Jim, 1958–
    Voices of the oral deaf : fourteen role models speak out /
Jim Reisler.
        p.   cm.
    Includes bibliographical references and index.
    ISBN 0-7864-1266-6 (softcover : 50# alkaline paper) ∞
    1. Deaf—United States.   2. Deaf—United States—Biography.
3. Deaf—Means of communication.   I. Title.
HV2545 .R45   2002
305.9'08162—dc21   2002004196

British Library cataloguing data are available

Manufactured in the United States of America

*McFarland & Company, Inc., Publishers
    Box 611, Jefferson, North Carolina 28640
    www.mcfarlandpub.com*

For Tobie and Julia, with love

Acknowledgments

"It takes a village."

Okay, it's a cliché, but it's true. Although my experience in the oral deaf world is only at seven years and counting, I have been fortunate to meet and get to know a remarkable group of people, all of them dedicated to bettering the lives of deaf people.

The staff at the League for the Hard of Hearing are among those people. So are Lois Heymann, my family's mentor; Lori Kogan; Josie Rowley; and friends at the Deafness Research Foundation.

But in terms of this project, my most enduring thanks go to the role models interviewed here. Their willingness to examine their own lives to help others did more than fill the pages of this volume; it taught me a great deal about being a better parent and a better person. For those things alone, I'll always be grateful.

Contents

Preface

In June 1995, my wife, Tobie, and I heard the words we will never forget: "Your daughter is deaf."

At the time, our daughter, Julia, was a week beyond her first birthday. We had suspected for several months that something was amiss: there was the day, several months before, when Tobie dropped some pots in the kitchen and Julia didn't turn around. Or the time when we were by the fire station in our town of Irvington, New York, when the alarm went off and Julia didn't respond.

Several times, we took Julia to the pediatrician, only to be told that she seemed fine. Once, the doctor rang a bell behind her and she happened to turn around. Deaf? Most of the traditional causes of deafness from meningitis and rubella have been practically wiped out, it was explained to us, leaving extraordinarily small odds that anything was wrong.

The story of a pediatrician's misdiagnosis is a common one for deaf people and their families. So is the initial denial, particularly on the part of extended family members. Maybe it's not really deafness, I remember family members telling us; maybe it's just a blockage. Don't accept the answer and take Julia around to different experts, we were told. Sooner or later, you'll find it's something different. Anything but deafness.

Maybe it was really an infection, we tried to convince ourselves. Maybe it was a blockage and she needed tubes. Perhaps she just wasn't paying attention. Deaf? That wasn't within our realm of understanding. We had never even known anyone who was deaf.

For the parents whose child is diagnosed, the questions are a little more basic: Will your child ever be able to live a mainstreamed life? Will he or she have friends and be contented? Be able to go to school and fit in?

Today, we know the answers: Yes, yes and yes again.

In our case, we got lucky. Precisely one day and some 40 telephone calls after Julia was diagnosed, Tobie had found the League for the Hard of Hearing in New York City. A not-for-profit New York organization, the "League," as it's known, has a remarkable track record in helping deaf youngsters get along and thrive in mainstream society.

Tobie and I plunged into the oral deaf world like eager graduate students. We got involved in parent groups, went to conferences and read everything we could on the issue. Along the way, we made a solid and supportive network of friends ranging from deaf adults to other families with deaf children and a gifted group of professionals, including audiologists and speech therapists. We had the good fortune of meeting some extraordinary people who are deaf—people making a real difference, raising families and working in the community, in spite of their deafness.

This book has the first-person stories of some of those men and women. They are the all-star team, all of them success stories with a collective wisdom from which all of us can learn. Evenly divided between men and women, they include a healthy dose of diversity and span from young adulthood to maturity. Some are single, some married, and some have children while others don't.

Above all, they represent a range of oral deaf experience, from those who were born deaf to those who became deaf as children or as teenagers. Their main connection: All use speech as their primary means of communication, although most do know sign language.

As a parent of a hearing-impaired youngster, I am awed by these people. Their practical advice, unwavering sense of optimism and commitment to helping others are inspiring. Sharing their stories has been a real help to my family and will continue to be so: Sure, parenthood is exhausting, but in re-reading these pieces, I know that everything is going to be okay.

Jump ahead nearly some six years from the day Julia was diagnosed. In 1997, she received a cochlear implant at a time when her vocabulary was no more than a few dozen words. Today, Julia has a vocabulary in the thousands, and, as a mainstreamed second grader, is a good student. Her social calendar is chock-full, and she reserves particular passion, in no special order, for art, her beagle puppy and two cats, the American Girl book series, gymnastics, Britney Spears, most things pink and the New York Yankees.

In other words (and with a nod to a justifiable degree of parental bias), Julia, at the age of nine, is a connected, interesting little person — so much so that I often try to step back to pinch myself when taking stock of how far she has come in such a short time.

A hearing colleague who read some of these interviews said her most lasting impression was that after a few pages, she stopped thinking of these people as having a physical handicap. That's the idea: They cease being regarded as deaf, but are understood as role models giving all of us a better comprehension of what it takes to succeed and lead productive lives in the mainstream.

Introduction

"It took seven days to create the world, it took us seven days to change it," was the joke, signed among Gallaudet University students back in 1988, when their protests successfully convinced the university's board of directors to appoint its first deaf president.

At the time, those students were euphoric: they had faced down the administration winning what became recognized in time as an important, symbolic victory for deaf rights. The standoff drew headlines around the world and was generally considered the birth of a movement called Deaf Culture, an expression of solidarity among deaf people emphasizing their right to sign and be treated as a culture and not as disabled.

Those students may have been joking, but their words spoke to a larger truth: the deaf world is a divisive, complicated one, torn by the allegiance of some people to the tenets of Deaf Culture, others to oralism and still others to a program called Total Communication, which emphasizes a combination of signing and speaking.

Hearing people are often surprised to learn of such divisions. Deafness isn't announced with a wheelchair or a set of crutches; in contrast, a hearing aid or the latest technological marvel, the cochlear implant, is either hard to see or not visible at all. Probably the most common reaction among the hearing to deafness is ignorance, with a tinge of anger; hearing is just something that people assume can be done in everyday life. So, when a person can't hear, it's often the speaker who reacts in anger. Not a nice thing to hear in this age of political correctness: "What are you? Deaf?" is a common, derogatory insult, used more than you think in television situation comedies.

The insults and inconveniences are everyday occurrences for deaf people. That may have been in part what motivated those students at Gallaudet; unused to getting their way, the students, by voicing their opinions, were expressing both the satisfaction at being heard and the anger at not being better understood. Multiply those difficulties by an entire lifetime and you can begin to get a sense of why many Deaf Culturists are sometimes hostile against mainstream hearing society.

Indeed, that divisiveness within deaf society has a long-standing historical legacy. Throughout most of the 19th century, the hand- and gesture-oriented language of sign or what became known in the U.S. as American Sign Language (ASL) was the preferred form of communication for the deaf. Then, in the late part of the 19th century, those tenets were challenged by none other than Alexander Graham Bell, the inventor of the telephone and the husband of a deaf woman. Bell believed that the deaf could speak.

Bell's theories were the roots of oralism, a belief that the best avenue for the deaf to communicate was through written, spoken and lip-read words. Bell's theories were grounded in the fundamental belief that deafness was a disability. He and his supporters labeled helping the deaf as "improving on nature" through technology like telephones and hearing aids. At the same time, they presented a darker side to the debate, supporting legislation to restrict marriage among the "socially unfit" and urging that deaf people get genetic testing to dissuade them from having children. They even sought to banish sign language and to have deaf children educated by learning to speak.

On the other hand, late-19th century advocates of sign like Laurent Clerc and Edward Gallaudet took a different view. They believed the major problem wasn't with the deaf, but with the hearing mainstream who only saw the deaf as impaired. Indeed, the series of debates that Clerc, Gallaudet and Bell had were the roots of the now century-old debate.

In recent years, that debate has turned particularly accusatory. Factions of Deaf Culturists accuse the oralists of trying to turn deaf children into speakers, therefore abandoning the deaf culture and setting their children up for a lifetime in which they'll be torn between signing and speaking. The oralists, in turn, accuse Deaf Culture advocates of being closed-minded and of ignoring the really strong academic performances of deaf children in mainstream schools.

Fueling the debate are technological improvements like high-powered hearing aids and a truly remarkable hearing device, the cochlear implant.

Indeed, oralists look to an era when the technology, aided by traditional speech therapy, will give all deaf children the opportunity to enter mainstream life. "Why not give these children all the advantages that hearing children have?" oralists argue.

Even the terminology is a minefield. For years, the deaf were cruelly called "deaf and dumb" there were many who assumed that deaf people may not have articulated as well as hearing people because they weren't intelligent enough. That term, thank goodness, isn't heard much anymore.

Today, the preference varies with the person. The most common term is probably just "deaf," although some prefer the lower case "d" for deaf, while others, usually Deaf Culturists, choose Deaf with an upper case "D." Some choose "hard of hearing" or "hearing impaired," terms despised by Deaf Culture because it implies that they and not the mainstream are the handicapped ones.

The cochlear implant is an extraordinary technological breakthrough. An electronic hearing device that is surgically inserted into the inner ear, the implant, at the minimum, can enable a deaf person to sense environmental sounds — a barking dog, a lawnmower or a honking horn. At the optimum, it can bring a deaf person into the mainstream and help them acquire speech.

Unlike a hearing aid, which amplifies sound, the implant actually feeds electronic impulses straight to the brain, doing the job of the damaged hair cells in the inner ear. Since its release, more than 14,000 of these devices have been surgically inserted into deaf people, most of whom are children.

And it's those children, most of them born to hearing parents, who have given the signing versus oralism debate its particular edge. Although the number of people implanted represent only four percent of all deaf people in the U.S., one deaf child in 10 has an implant. And projections suggest that in the next decade, the ratio will climb to one in three.

Deaf Culture advocates say those children will grow to be in a kind of limbo — banished by science from deaf culture and never really accepted in the mainstream hearing world. They say that young children are implanted for the benefit of the parents only and, at the very least, the children should have the option of making the decision to implant.

Some of the more militant members of Deaf Culture recommend that deaf children be raised by the deaf community and actually be taken away from their hearing parents to live in a silent world. They compare implanting a deaf child to genocide of a culture and suggest it is akin to changing somebody because he or she has blond hair or speaks French.

Oralists point to countless success stories, particularly children, many of them with implants, who attend regular schools and are a part of hearing society. Those children, they say, do well in schools, play sports, have active social lives and will go on to college.

The controversy continues. So do success stories among the oral deaf, including the people you will meet here. All are accomplished, grounded people who faced a substantial challenge early in life and have triumphed. Moreover, they are an involved group with a true commitment to community service and to helping the families of deaf children.

Deaf Culturists will argue that these people are the achievers and thus the exception. If that's the case, so be it: They have so much to share.

Kristin Buehl

WASHINGTON, D.C.

After graduating from Princeton University with a B.A. in History in 1999, Kristin Buehl moved to Washington, D.C., where she is a paralegal specialist at the U.S. Department of Justice. Buehl works in the Civil Rights Division, Criminal Section, where she assists in investigating and prosecuting criminal conduct involving deprivations of federal civil rights, including racial and religious violence, misconduct by law enforcement officers, violations of peonage and involuntary servitude statutes and violence against reproductive health care facilities. She plans to attend law school in the near future.

❧

On top of my bookcase back at college, I kept a framed quote from Helen Keller, my heroine, that goes like this: "So much has been given to me; I have no time to ponder that which has been denied."

I admire Helen Keller and try to emulate her. The fact that she was deaf and blind and accomplished so much is extraordinary. Can you imagine? It puts into context the fact that I'm only deaf. I look at her and think that I can accomplish things, too.

I was born profoundly deaf. No one knows why I'm deaf because there's no sign of it anywhere in my family. My mom noticed that I wasn't talking as an infant, so she took me to a doctor who said there was nothing wrong with me. He told her not to worry about it.

As time passed, my mother kept telling the doctor that she thought something was wrong with my hearing. He continued to say that he thought my hearing was fine. Finally, when I was 15 months old, she took me to a new doctor and insisted that something was wrong. Although that doctor said she thought my hearing was fine, at my mother's insistence she referred us to an ear, nose and throat specialist who concurred with my mother. Soon afterward, I was given a formal hearing test that confirmed that I had a profound hearing loss. I was 16 months old.

By the time I was 18 months old, I was fitted with two hearing aids. I didn't like them at first. I'd take them off and throw them against the wall. I think I must have been shocked at hearing noise for the first time.

As soon as my parents learned that I was deaf, they began reading a lot about deafness and deaf education and began looking at schools for me in the San Francisco Bay area, where we lived at the time. They didn't know if I should be educated orally or via total communication, but were impressed by the results obtained by a private oral school south of San Francisco. Many of its graduates were successfully mainstreamed. Based on my mother's observations at various schools, it just didn't appear possible to do both manual and oral communication well simultaneously.

Usually it was the oral communication that suffered when both were taught. Also, my parents felt that I could learn sign language later. So, I ended up at an oral pre-school south of San Francisco, requiring an hour drive each way to get there. But my mother says it was worth it because I was learning to talk.

A year later, when I was two-and-a-half, my parents got divorced, so my mom, younger sister and I moved to western Massachusetts to be near my mother's relatives and the Clarke School for the Deaf. I entered the Clarke School when I was three years old and really loved it. I had the best time there because everybody around me was deaf and I had the best social life. Also, the academics were very strong and my self-confidence and self-image were greatly enhanced.

But, while my social life and self image were good, one of the disadvantages at Clarke was that there wasn't much exposure to people who weren't deaf or who weren't educators of the deaf. It was easy there: Everything was closed-captioned and everybody talked slowly and faced you when they spoke. Same thing when I went home: My mom and sister, who are hearing, spoke slowly, so communication was never a problem.

Then my mom remarried and I got two stepsisters. I had to start learning how to socialize more with hearing people. My sisters would bring their friends over and I learned how to communicate with them.

While it's important for any deaf child to have deaf friends, at the same time it's very, very important for that child to be with hearing people and be comfortable around them, especially at a young age.

Don't get me wrong: I loved Clarke and would recommend it to anyone. But a lot of my friends boarded there and didn't have much exposure to the "real world" of hearing people. The fact that I was a day student meant I went home every night to the hearing world, which made a big difference in my ability to learn how to speak and interact with hearing people.

Kristin Buehl

There were people who graduated from Clarke after completing eighth grade who were shocked when they mainstreamed into regular high schools. They couldn't take it and transferred to schools for the deaf and or later went to Gallaudet University where signing is the preferred form of communication. Some deaf students who don't have any hearing friends aren't prepared for the real hearing world.

I've seen the opposite happen as well. I have a deaf friend who was fully mainstreamed in "hearing" schools through eighth grade, when I met her. I was the first deaf person she had ever met. She was amazed to see how wonderful it was to have a deaf friend. Then she had a strong reaction — dropping out of her hearing school, looking into Deaf Culture and transferring to a school for the deaf. That's what happens sometimes to some deaf people who were never previously exposed to other deaf people. In contrast, I have some deaf friends who were mainstreamed all of their lives and don't regret it for a minute.

The point I want to make is that I was raised belonging to both the deaf world and the hearing world. You need to be part of both, especially at a young age, so you won't feel like you missed out on anything and you can make well-informed choices. My mom always made sure I was exposed to both sides.

After I completed the third grade at Clarke, my family moved to McLean, Virginia, outside Washington, D.C. My mother faced a new decision: either let me board at Clarke or attend a regular school as a mainstreamed student. It was difficult because, at the time, my whole life was the Clarke School. I ended up in Virginia where we found a regular elementary school with a special program for oral hearing impaired children.

It was hard leaving my friends at Clarke. On the other hand, I've always been the type of person who likes trying new things and meeting new people, so it wasn't bad. Plus, I had my sister, and, by then, two stepsisters, so if I didn't make any new friends, I always had family.

Three years later when I finished elementary school, my mother faced another big decision: determining where I should go to school for junior high. Should I return to Clarke as a boarding student or fully mainstream in a private (hearing) school or continue in the oral public school program as a partially mainstreamed student? She decided I would fully mainstream in a private school because she thought I was ready to face the challenges of being fully mainstreamed.

Seventh grade, however, was really tough. Here I was mainstreaming for the first time and many of my classmates had never even met a deaf person before and they were confused about my speech. They didn't know what to make of me; they didn't know at first that I was deaf. Then word got around. The reaction was, "Oh, my God, she's deaf! … Oh, my God!"

That's a hard age anyway. You're reaching puberty and it tends to be very cliquish. Everybody worries about his or her looks. And so I had a hard time making friends in seventh grade. I didn't speak as well then as I do now and a lot of people just didn't understand me. In hindsight, I realize that up to this point, I hadn't put much effort into improving my speech. In an environment in which everybody is deaf, you can use "deaf speech" and consequently, you don't have to try as hard. But in a mainstream environment, I realized that I had to work harder — in my studies, making friends and articulating speech.

Seventh grade was the first and only time that I was embarrassed to be deaf and wished that I could be hearing so I could be like other people. I had a hard time being accepted and I didn't do as well academically as I had previously. I pretended to be hearing. I wore my hair down all the time to hide my hearing aids and never talked in class. When a teacher called on me, I'd shrug and say, "I don't know," because I didn't want to talk in front of others. When I had to give an oral report, I would call in sick and not go to school. I didn't want people to hear me talk "with a funny accent" and perhaps make fun of me.

Then one day in eighth grade, I realized that that attitude was ridiculous. Here's what happened: A third grade teacher in my school asked me to talk about my deafness in front of his class. I was petrified because I thought people would hear me and make fun of my speech. But then I thought, "What have I got to lose?" After all, the teacher assured me, "They're just little kids."

So, I spoke to his class. I brought my TDD [telecommunications device for the deaf] and showed them my hearing aids. Their jaws dropped. They were interested and I realized that these kids thought being deaf was pretty cool. That was important. I remember thinking, "They think I'm pretty neat" and I started to grow in confidence. It was at that point that I realized that I was deaf and I had no choice but to embrace it.

All the time, my mom was there, pulling for me and telling me that I could do it. I have a good analogy: In college, I remember in psychology studying Freud, whose mother told herself at his birth that he was going to be a great man someday. So, every time somebody crossed her path, she'd stop that person and tell them what a great man her son would be someday. Freud himself came to believe it, too. My mother is like Freud's mother: She believes and tells me that I'm an extraordinary person who will do amazing things one day. Sure, there are times when I doubt her, but she says it so often that I've learned to believe it.

And that, I think, is the best way to raise a deaf child or any child for that matter. Tell them they can do it. My mom did and I started to do better academically and gain confidence in high school. I was still nervous around hearing people and didn't always think I was as good as many of my classmates. I knew that I was successful compared to other deaf people, but compared to hearing people, I still wasn't so sure.

In the meantime, my grandfather wrote me occasionally and gave me all sorts of inspiration. His life motto is "Attitude plus Effort equal Success." He told me stories about people who became a success after going through hardship. He would write to me and say, "Krissy, did you know that Abraham Lincoln was defeated in public office five times before he was elected the President of the United States?" And, "Did you know that Babe Ruth struck out more than anyone else in baseball history, yet broke all the records for home runs?" I will never forget my grandfather's immortal words: "Never, never give up."

I did amazingly well in high school. I went to a private school, the Potomac School in my hometown of McLean, VA. The smaller class sizes and individualized attention paid off. I was also involved in all kinds of activities — particularly in sports, where I achieved some success. I played tennis, made the varsity basketball team as a freshman and played lacrosse so well that I was selected for a national team. Being a good athlete has its advantages; people were always coming up to me and wanting to talk about the game. It helped me prove myself in the hearing world.

I was also very involved in the school's community service club, which forced me to interact with people. That proves another thing — you have to be active because it's the only way to meet people. Waiting for others to come up to you doesn't work because, typically, people won't do that, particularly if you're deaf. You have to make yourself visible and show the world that you're capable of doing anything. By the end of high school, I had been there long enough that people started seeing me not as a deaf woman, but as Kristin Buehl.

And all the time, there was my mom, going to see my teachers, advocating for my needs in the classroom, always making sure they were aware of things like facing me when they spoke. She's really something and I give her a lot of credit for who I am today.

A lot of it just comes down to the fact that you have to be positive. I've learned to always have a positive outlook on life because it's the only way to survive.

Applying to Princeton was Mom's idea. I didn't think I had a shot, but she made me apply. Eighteen people from my high school class applied and only three were accepted. Guess who was the only girl accepted? Yup. Me.

College was harder than high school in some ways and easier in others. Academically, it was so much easier. One reason was because I'd developed excellent study habits in high school. I had to study harder than most in high school because I got so little out of class. Lip-reading class discussions and most lectures was nearly impossible. As a result, I was self-taught from textbooks and my friends' class notes. It's a given that I know how to study hard. Perhaps, then, I was better prepared for college than many of my classmates.

Another reason academics were easier for me in college was the support services I had that I never received in high school. Looking back, I missed a lot of the lectures and classroom discussion in high school, whereas in college, for the first time, I didn't miss a thing. The reason is Real Time Captioning or RTC, which enabled me to understand almost every single word in class. RTC is a system that enabled me to read on a laptop computer screen everything being said in class. A former court reporter attends class with me and transcribes everything. I didn't have to borrow notes from friends anymore and I could even take my own notes.

Another reason it was easier in college than high school was that my speech had improved and I'm easier to understand. I meet people who hear the way I talk and it never occurs to them that I might possibly be deaf. They had never met a deaf person before and they would ask me where I'm from. They asked me, "I know you're not from France or Germany or Spain, but really, where are you from?" When I would tell them I was deaf and that was a deaf accent, they'd be really surprised and ask, "How can you even hear or understand me?" I'd explain and it was like a whole new world to them.

Another factor was that my peers in college were more mature and receptive. College was a lot of fun. You see and meet so many different people and you learn from them. And Princeton was quite a place: In high school, you had smart people and average people, whereas in college, everybody was at the top of his or her class in high school. I had so much respect for them.

The thing is, though, I fit in at Princeton. I didn't find a lot of people in high school who shared interests similar to mine, in part because there were only 60 people in my class. I tended to hang around the same people all the time. But in college, there was a lot of variety and diversity, of which I was a part. I fit into the diversity there.

Not only were my peers more mature in college than they were in high school, I had grown more confident and independent by then. In high school, I was very dependent on my two best friends. They were always interpreting conversations for me and were always there to take notes. Plus, my mom wasn't at college to talk to the professors about deafness, the way she was there for me in high school. In college, I was entirely on my own, and it was up to me to speak for myself.

I changed a lot in college. I became more confident about acknowledging my deafness and encouraging people to be more comfortable around me. Being outgoing seemed to work the best in setting fellow students at ease. I learned that most hearing students simply weren't going to go out of their way to introduce themselves to a deaf person, because they often didn't know what to expect and worried whether they'd be able to understand me.

In addition, having a captioner in my classes clearly made a difference in how the students viewed me; it left some afraid, some curious, and some confused. That's why I think it's so crucial for a deaf person to have an outgoing personality — to go up to people and initiate the conversation, as a way to show them that she or he is not just a stone statuette silently sitting in front of the captioner (or interpreter). Being personable can break the ice or initial nervousness any hearing student might have if they never met or shared a class with a deaf student before.

While engaging in conversation, I always make sure to talk about my deafness. In college, once the hearing students realized that I didn't think being deaf was a big deal, they felt more comfortable asking me questions about my deafness. Believe me, most of them were fascinated by and wanted to know all about it. That allowed people to get to know me and I them. Ironically, as we got to know each other, they eventually didn't care or seem to notice that I was deaf because they realized that I was just as normal as they were.

Still, the beginning of college was a really rough time. As a freshman, I struggled to find deeper friendships, despite the greater scope of friends and classmates to choose from compared to high school. Not only that, but my freshman roommate made it difficult for me to get off to a good start in college. She was one of those people who was always worried about what others thought of her. She was embarrassed she had a roommate who was deaf. I look back now and say to myself, "That's her problem." But I didn't see it at the time and let her intimidate me.

I recall the beginning of my freshman year, when I was frustrated for not yet having built friendships similar to what I had in high school. I remember thinking a lot about whether I was doing the right thing being mainstreamed in a regular college where I was the only deaf student on campus. And I remember conversations with my Gallaudet University friends, who would always say they were having the best time there partying and making friends instantaneously.

Yet, here I was, just trying to make friends and asking myself, "Why am I here?" and "Why am I doing this?" and "It would be so much easier attending a college for deaf students." But looking back, I know that route wasn't me. Fortunately, before going to college, I was exposed to life on a deaf college campus, since I grew up in McLean, which is outside Washington, D.C., Gallaudet's home.

During my high school years, I used to go to Gallaudet and Model

Secondary School for the Deaf (the high school on Gallaudet's campus) and socialize with other deaf people. I got a sense of what Deaf Culture was like and never had any desire to go there. I knew I wanted to choose another path, so I stuck it out during my freshman year at Princeton.

I realize now that I made the best decision ever. In fact, things got so much better at the beginning of sophomore year, especially when I got more active, such as participating in student government and volunteering for community service projects. It was then that I was allowed to pick roommates and live in a suite with five of my friends: I had a blast and I wouldn't have traded it for anywhere else.

I also realize that I wasn't the only freshman who found the first year of college difficult. You meet a lot of people who hated their freshman year and like college much better after that. College is a huge adjustment: You have to make new friends and you don't have your family there. I realize now that I was dependent on them and that good friendships take time to build.

In a sense, I sometimes feel like I'm on a mission. I'm here to teach people about deafness. After all, so much has been given to me that I want to pass it on and give it back. No matter where I end up, one thing is for sure: I'll always have a voice for myself.

My deafness has been a gift. If it had not been for my deafness, I would be a different person today and I wouldn't want to change myself for anything in the world. Because of my deafness, I have learned to be strong, confident and unconquerable, especially in the face of discouragement and frustration. My deafness has given me many extraordinary experiences that only a few get to encounter, and I can only look forward to the many more that are about to come. It has been quite an adventure!

Tom Fields

GAITHERSBURG, MARYLAND

Tom Fields is an architect with the National Park Service, with a specialty in historic preservation and contemporary architecture. He graduated with honors from the University of Maryland School of Architecture and received the university's Outstanding Alumnus Award in 1990. A graduate of Clarke School for the Deaf, Fields is a member of its board of trustees.

He has served as chairperson of the Deaf and Hard of Hearing Section (formerly the Oral Hearing Impaired Section), a part of the Alexander Graham Bell Association for the Deaf and Hard of Hearing. Fields has written numerous articles on behalf of A.G. Bell, which he has represented at congressional and other legislative hearings.

❧

I am a native of Montgomery County, Maryland, just outside of Washington, D.C. I spent 12 of my first 16 years away from home. My brother, Mickey, who is also deaf, and I were sent away to the Clarke School for the Deaf in Northampton, Massachusetts.

I arrived at Clarke in 1950. For my parents, it was a choice between sending us there or to the Maryland School for the Deaf. They decided to send us to Clarke because they felt that we had a better chance of learning to speak for ourselves and acquiring a good education. Mickey preceded me at Clarke by a couple of years. When we went to school, our parents didn't leave Maryland to be with us, because my father already had an established dental practice.

At first, being away from home was very traumatic and painful. I was only four-and-a-half years old. I still remember that very first night at Clarke, when I realized that my parents were not coming back for me. I suddenly felt homesick and cried all night. The dorm counselor, who took me under her wing along with other little boys far from home, had to rock me to sleep.

The feeling of homesickness went on for a few more nights. But over time, I got used to living away from home. I started making new friends among other boys and girls in my first class. Clarke was, and still is,

Tom Fields

an excellent school with a beautiful campus. At school I never thought of myself as being different — I was among other deaf children, kids like me.

After eighth grade, I started high school in my hometown — Walt Whitman High School, in Bethesda. By then I was 16, and I had gone through a bumpy transition. I think that was because I was a bit immature and didn't yet know how to co-exist with hearing peers. I was brought up at Clarke School for 12 years and had never had the chance to learn to get along with hearing people day in and day out. After Clarke, I was immediately placed at a high school of approximately 3,000 hearing students. I was the only deaf person in my class; there were two other deaf students in other grades. Of those two, one graduated and one dropped out.

Being a teenager can be difficult for anybody, deaf or hearing. In school, I had to take the initiative in certain class situations to help make things easier for myself. I always sat in the front row and I made sure the teacher faced the class when talking. Also, I asked them to make carbon copies of class notes for me.

❧

My high school years weren't all that easy. I had to work hard and simply try the best I could. You might consider me "book smart," but I missed a lot during class discussions. Today, many mainstreamed deaf and hard-of-hearing students have access to interpreters and Computer-Assisted Real Time captioning (CART). I didn't have the benefit of these. If I'd had interpreters, perhaps I wouldn't have had to study as hard. On the other hand, I might have thought it too easy and been inattentive in class.

I always thought school was difficult, so I studied hard, very hard, in high school. My efforts began to pay off when I realized that some of my classmates were getting Cs, while I was getting As and Bs. So it was reassuring to discover that I really was doing okay academically.

As for my social and extracurricular life in high school, I was involved in sports — football, wrestling, and track and field. I didn't go out much — not because I was deaf, but because I was shy and didn't date a lot.

What helped me a lot back then was something I took with me from my years at Clarke — having deaf and hard-of-hearing adult role models. The Clarke School alumni occasionally came to campus to talk to us, and I looked up to those alumni. I vividly recall one time when I was sick in the infirmary, and the president of the Clarke School Alumni Association took the time to come in to talk with me. She encouraged me to get better and then to do well in school.

Another time, I had the good fortune to meet a deaf architect who had graduated from Clarke. Did he have any influence on my becoming an architect? I can't say for sure, but maybe he did. All I know is that I really appreciated those contacts. What a great experience, for all of us kids at Clarke, to meet deaf and hard-of-hearing adults who had successful careers and fulfilling lives! Beginning at a very early age, my encounters with these people gave me adult role models to try to emulate, as well as a sense of identity as I grew up. These kinds of meetings would be a positive and informative experience for any new parents of deaf and hard-of-hearing children, but even more so for the children themselves. I know it had a positive impact on me.

After high school, college didn't seem all that difficult, at least at first. I guess that was because I didn't have classes all day, like I did in high school. I went to Franklin and Marshall College in Lancaster, Pennsylvania, with the hope of majoring in pre-med. That's where I flunked a course for the first time in my life — chemistry. The professor had a bad attitude and was unwilling to work with me to resolve my difficulty with following class discussions and lectures.

Ironically, he was himself disabled. He had problems with his back that kept him from standing up straight. I had a difficult time understanding him because he was talking to the floor most of the time. I didn't ask for lots of concessions, but he refused to make any at all. He would not help me resolve the problem. So, having no idea what was going on in the course, I had a rough time.

Obviously, pre-med was not going to pan out for me. However, I was good with my hands, so I thought of majoring in Fine Arts. But my father got on my case, wondering what I was going to do with that kind of degree. (He said I would have to get master's and doctorate degrees and then end up teaching art.) So then I said to myself, "Okay, why not architecture?" Again, I'd always been "book smart," and that, along with my manual dexterity, made architecture seem like a good fit for me.

I transferred to the University of Maryland School of Architecture. The architectural classes were small; during my first year, there were 50 of us. Then, 40 more joined us the following year, making it a class of 90. But it was tough; by the time we graduated, there were only 19 of us. As in high school, English and history were problematic for me because I couldn't follow class discussions. Courses like physics and calculus, on the other hand, were not problematic because discussions among students weren't required.

My architecture courses sometimes presented obstacles. For instance, I couldn't follow what instructors or other students were saying in their presentations because they often included overhead displays or slides, which were presented with the lights off. To make things even more difficult, notetakers and interpreters were not available.

It was difficult, but I managed to get by; architectural technology, design and structural engineering were not all that bad. For the most part, what the instructors had to say was already included in the textbooks or handouts. Also, I made a point to get on the "good side" of the instructors at the beginning of each year, explaining that I could not hear so they could give me the extra attention I needed.

❧

I graduated with honors in 1972. I worked for a private architectural firm for two years before joining the National Park Service (NPS) in 1974. I worked for the Denver Service Center (DSC), a division within the National Park Service that provides professional support for the Parks — architectural and engineering design, planning and construction of a wide range of projects. Specifically, I specialized in historic preservation and contemporary architecture.

While with DSC, which oversaw a lot of multidisciplinary projects, I had the opportunity to work as a project architect on jobs ranging from the rehabilitation of the seawalls and Star Fort at Fort McHenry National Monument in Baltimore to the construction and restoration work at the Harpers Ferry and C&O Canal National Historic Parks in West Virginia, as well as at many other locations in and around Washington, D.C.

For several years, before switching over to construction management, I was an architectural-engineering (A-E) manager for several projects, including the rehabilitation of the Lincoln and Jefferson Memorials. I was also the A-E manager for the development of the George Washington Memorial Parkway Maintenance Facility near Reagan National Airport in Northern Virginia.

During my earlier years with DSC (prior to 1987), I realized that in order to be more involved with contemporary architectural design, I had to work in construction as a project inspector or construction manager for a couple of years. So I applied for a detail in construction in the Washington, D.C., area. My request for such a detail was met with a lot of resistance from the management because of my deafness. They were concerned for my safety. They didn't realize that I had worked in residential construction during my high school and college days (I worked for a plumber and a roofing company for several summers). Because of the management's unwillingness to give me the opportunity, I had to explain to them that what they were doing was discriminatory. They found me a job as a project inspector. They tried to do it locally in the Washington area, but the chief of the construction branch in the area was not willing to take me on board. Instead of pushing the issue with this particular person, the management found someone out West more willing to take me on board.

As a result I got the job as a project inspector for the construction of a maintenance facility (with a budget of $5.5 million) in Sequoia National Park during 1987 and 1988. This opportunity turned out to be one of the best times in my career with the NPS and my personal life. My family lived in Kings Canyon National Park while I was working in Sequoia National Park. While there, we visited many places, mostly national parks in California and Nevada.

In Sequoia, I did not have immediate access to the interpreting services to which I was entitled for my job. Since the project was located deep in the Sierra Nevadas — a good two-hour drive from fair-sized cities such as Fresno and Visalia — I did not feel it was justifiable to have an interpreter drive up to interpret for a short time and then drive back. For reasons like this, I feel very fortunate to be able to speak for myself.

Telephone communication in Sequoia was never a major issue. To facilitate telephone communications, I loaned the contractor a telecommunication device for the deaf (TTY), and the main office obtained several for use by me and others in that office. To further improve communication access, the main office took advantage of my deafness to justify acquiring fax machines, new technology at that time.

After working there for less than a year, I became the construction manager of the project. Upon its successful completion, my family and I headed back home.

Due to a big decrease in design work, I eventually had to switch over to the construction branch. I worked as the project supervisor on three major construction projects: the rehabilitation of historic structures in Fort Wadsworth in New York City; the replacement of the roof at the White House; and the rehabilitation of the visitor center at the Jefferson Memorial.

Because of a mandatory reduction in the workforce at the Denver Service Center, I transferred to the National Capital Region in Washington, D.C. Currently, I am working as the project supervisor, monitoring various construction projects in the Washington Metropolitan area, which I've done for the last three years. These projects include small jobs, such as replacing the roofs of NPS properties (with a budget of about $20,000), to large projects, such as the exterior rehabilitation of Ford's Theater in Washington, D.C. ($450,000), and the rehabilitation and addition in the United States Park Police Headquarters at the George Washington Memorial Parkway ($1.4 million).

My job has always been challenging, but with the use of interpreters and the advent of technology like e-mail, voice carry-overs, on-line instant messaging and faxes, my ability to communicate has become easier and my responsibilities have increased. If I have a staff meeting with more than four or five people, I use an interpreter. With e-mail, I can communicate with just about anyone, anytime.

Although technology has improved communication for me, my career has not been without other obstacles. When I applied for a position at the White House as an architect in 1988, like many deaf people, I experienced discrimination in the workplace for the first time. A person far less qualified than me was given the position. I found out later that one of the three evaluators had graded me proportionally lower than the rest. While I lodged a complaint to try and give the bureaucracy a "wake-up call," I did not allow the situation to consume my time and prevent me from moving ahead in other areas of my career.

I know sign language well enough to get by with other deaf people, having learned when I was 30. I learned it in order to socialize with friends who can't speak or speech-read well. Socializing with hearing people requires work. I work all day with hearing people, communicating orally. So at home with the family — my wife, Barb, and our two boys, Ryan, 18, and Aaron, 15 — we use a mixture of both signs and speech. It is more relaxing that way. Really, who wants to work to have fun?

I also have a son and a daughter from a previous marriage. They're both out of college. Andy is married and lives in the state of Washington. He works for Intel. Sarabeth lives in Framingham, Massachusetts, and works for Harvard Business School Publishing. I use e-mail or on-line instant messaging to communicate with them all the time. And since my cochlear implant, inserted and activated in the spring of 1999, I am starting to have even short telephone conversations with them. The first time I tried it, I was calling my daughter to get the zip code of her address. I am still in therapy twice a week, at the Johns Hopkins Listening Center and on my own with a friend. I continue to make progress on that front.

My involvement in community issues for the deaf was generated by this one fact: I am concerned that deaf children do not get a fair shake in our society without the opportunity to learn to speak and speech-read. My hope is for deaf children to be able to speak for themselves. I'm not opposed to learning and using sign language, as long as they also try to learn how to speak. Being able to speak for myself has been fundamental to my success in life.

Parents should become informed and keep their minds open to all available options and opportunities so their children can do everything possible to achieve success. Love and support is vital, too, when a young deaf or hard-of-hearing person begins to make his or her own decisions. If a child gets a cochlear implant at an early age and then decides not to use it later in life, I don't think this decision should be treated as a setback, but as a change in personal direction. Because of the possibility of life-changing decisions such as this, I strongly believe that those who learn to use their residual hearing to the maximum or have a cochlear implant should also learn to speech-read.

To this end, it's important for parents to include their deaf or hard-of-hearing children in conversations during meal times and other occasions. My parents made the mistake of not including my brother and me in their conversations. Times were different then — maybe they didn't realize what an important skill it would be. We had to work that much harder to hone our speaking and speech-reading skills on our own.

❧

Those of us concerned about today's deaf and hard-of-hearing children must understand that education utilizing the oral method may not be for everyone. We need to realize that every single child is different and each has a different need. I try to tell parents to be aware of other options and to keep an open mind about the possibility of changing to different modes of communication.

Sadly, the oral method is not a cure-all, and neither are other options. There is no right or wrong in this. It's important for parents to be willing to learn a different mode of communication — signing or a combination of both or even cued-speech and they should not fear or resist change. For instance, when I considered getting the cochlear implant, I realized that the odds were great that I would still not be able to talk on the phone, but I went ahead with it. Now, I am learning to use the telephone on a limited basis.

Some professional proponents of the oral method say that if a child learns to sign, he or she will never learn to speak. My experience proves otherwise. I know of a few deaf individuals who learned to sign first and now speak very well for themselves. That is due to the direct involvement and hard work of parents. I feel it is an injustice if children are not given a chance to learn to speak for themselves. They should be provided with the method of communication that is most suitable for them.

However, parents have the right to make their own decisions on how their deaf and hard-of-hearing children communicate. Becoming informed and weighing every option is the key. If they choose the oral method for their children — well, I think that's great. If they want their children to learn to sign, I respect that too. I take exception to people who try to tell parents what to do, and it happens on both sides of the issue.

Personally, as a parent, I simply cannot tolerate those who try to dictate to parents what's best for their children, be it oral communication or signing. There are some deaf people in the community trying to convince new parents that their deaf or hard-of-hearing children *must* learn to sign, and that the care and education of those children should be the responsibilities *solely* of deaf adults.

A few years ago, I gave a commencement address at Clarke. Like volunteering my time to the Alexander Graham Bell Association for the Deaf, I call it "give-back time." When I was first asked to give the address, I remember thinking, "I'm no public speaker." Then I decided to ignore that trepidation and just give it my best shot. Sharing the success I've had in my career will hopefully convince, and inspire, deaf and hard-of-hearing students to reach for their goals too.

Today, young deaf and hard-of-hearing people are indeed pushing the envelope farther than my generation did. When I was in college, I didn't have the benefit of interpreters and advanced technology. Now, with technology and legislation favoring all disabled people, young people are achieving more than was ever dreamed of during my younger days.

In spite of what I have accomplished, I am not unique. There are many other deaf and hard-of-hearing individuals out there who are doing just as well or better. I hope we can all set an example for the deaf and hard-of-hearing children who follow us.

Jeff Float

Ranco Mirage, California

Jeff Float is an Olympic gold medalist, having swum the third leg on the United States 4×200 meter freestyle relay team at the 1984 Olympic Games in Los Angeles. A graduate of the University of Southern California and the 1984 captain of the U.S. Men's Swimming Team, he is thought to be the first hearing-impaired athlete to win a gold medal in the Olympic Games.

Float began swimming lessons at the age of three after his mother tired of him "chasing the family dog" around the house. Competing for the Arden Hills Swimming and Tennis Club in California, he won his first national title at the age of 10. Before he was done with swimming, Float was a four-year All-American in both high school and college and a U.S. national and world champion.

In the Olympic final, Float swam four laps, giving teammate and anchor swimmer Bruce Hayes a body length and a half (10 feet) lead. Hayes hit the water seconds before West German superstar Michael Gross who quickly shortened the distance between the two. But Hayes, swimming his last 10 meters without coming up for air, held on and edged out Gross by four-hundredths of a second. It was, in the words of Swimming World *magazine, "the most spectacular race in the Olympic Games (that year)."*

The victory did more than make up for Float's earlier disappointment of finishing fourth in the 200 freestyle, which Gross won. It set a world record and touched off an emotional victory celebration at the Olympic pool, where Float had competed for U.S.C. "You ever try to sleep with a smile on your face?" he said a day or two after the race, with the gold medal still draped around his neck. "Well, it's impossible."

In 1987, Float received his real estate license. Today he manages 20 single family homes for absentee owners and coaches the Laguna Creek Gators swim team for age group, six to 16. He is a frequent motivational speaker.

∾

The 1984 Olympic final was the first time I ever heard the crowd during a meet. On the other hand, it was the first time I had told myself to really listen for the crowd, and believe me, when there are 15,000 people at the pool screaming, you hear a roar. By swimming a lot, I always had people yelling for me: I always appreciated it, but being deaf, I learned to see it and feel it, as opposed to hearing it.

I'm fortunate to have found swimming. It was my thing. It was a focus that gave me a lot of extra benefits as I grew older, from traveling the world to the satisfaction and confidence from being on the best teams, having it pay for my college education, and, of course, being an Olympic gold medalist.

So when did I hang up the Speedo and retire? In 1984 at the age of 24. I had done all I could in my sport and reached the pinnacle. When you climb Mt. Everest, you don't have to find another mountain to climb.

My swimming career stems, in part, from being a California kid. I was born in Buffalo, New York, where I had meningitis and lost my hearing as a one-year-old. My dad was going to medical school at the time and when he graduated from the University of Buffalo, he got a job in Sacramento and we moved there.

∾

I got meningitis at 13 months of age. When I was sick, there was a kid in the next room at the hospital who died from the same thing. For me, it was a case of either dying or using the drugs that helped me recover, but the illness took away my hearing. I had a 105-degree temperature for a time, and was so hot that I was practically burning up. My parents tell me that they put me in an ice bath for a time and put me on a board and held me down so I wouldn't thrash in discomfort from the pain.

But I consider myself one of the fortunate ones: Instead of losing all of my hearing as many did, I lost about 90 percent in my right ear and 50-to-60 percent in my left ear. My parents didn't know right away; back then, there were no ways of accurately measuring hearing loss, and it wasn't until we were out in California that they could tell from certain behaviors at a certain age that something was wrong. They tell me that I was doing things like sitting right in front of the stereo speakers, repeating other people's words and just generally being kind of quiet.

A close friend of my mom's was an ear, nose and throat specialist who started noticing some of those "quiet" behaviors. And so, at the age of about three or four, they really realized that I had a hearing impairment and I was aided with a body aid. I remember going to kindergarten in one of the body aids with the hearing device strapped onto the chest and chords extending to both ears. No, it wasn't the most comfortable thing to wear.

Jeff Float

I started out in an elementary school special education program with other handicapped kids. My special education classes weren't just for hard of hearing children, and the school really wasn't equipped with the adaptive devices to help me. But my mother was a strong advocate of working with the local school board and politicians to upgrade the facility, so when they weren't able to do that, she decided to move me and go the mainstream route.

Mainstreaming started in second grade after my kindergarten and first grade years in which my mother wasn't content with how the system was working. She said to them, "I can do better; watch me." And so she set about to doing a lot of things on her own to make sure that I would get the best education possible: arranging for special speech therapists, lip reading class and a lot of one-on-one after school sessions.

Basically, my mom made sure I got a lot of extra steps that most kids just don't get. She became my advocate, which was a necessity. It's something I'm very thankful for today: My mom was always progressive in pursuing what was best for me and my dad is a doctor, an anesthesiologist, so he had a lot of overall awareness of the medical issues I faced as a hearing-impaired child.

Even so, I remember second grade being pretty difficult. I was at a new mainstreamed school and very unsure of how I'd do and how I'd fit in. I remember classmates looking at hearing aids and always asking me, "What are those?" and "What's that in your ears?" Kind of typical questions.

∿

Swimming really helped me fit in. I started swimming around second or third grade for the Arden Hills Swim Club, a local club about two miles from home. It's the club where well-known Olympians like Debbie Meyer, Mike Burton and Mark Spitz trained. It so happened that when I was learning how to swim there, the club coach, Sherm Chavoor, was revolutionizing distance swimming. So here I was, just a little pip-squeak at the time, but fortunate to find a peer group there and a group of people who, through competition, helped me thrive.

Swimming gave me confidence. Growing up, I always seemed to have that natural athletic ability — being able to pick up a football and be good at it, or play basketball and be good. Swimming was the same; a way to do something I could be good at and not have to hear. I could immerse myself in water, which is different from dry land. It was a different world and it was something I could do better than most others. I was just kind of a fish. I loved the water.

As a kid, I had a pretty well-rounded exposure to different activities. It wasn't just swimming; I was in Cub Scouts and Boy Scouts and played Little League baseball, where my passion was pitching. In junior high school, I played basketball and football as well. Then, as a high school freshman, I remember pitching in a senior league baseball championship game on the day before a section swimming championship: I pitched a one-hitter and won, but the next day, I didn't swim well at all because I was just too tired.

It was then that my swim coach pulled me aside and suggested I specialize — that is, dedicate myself to one sport or another. He told me that if I chose swimming, I could make the Olympic team someday. He thought I had the potential to do so.

Jesuit, my high school, is an all-boys, private Catholic prep school in Carmichael, with a reputation in academics and as an athletic powerhouse. At the time, my coach was urging me to choose the "swimming only" approach, my parents were of the attitude that I should try all kinds of things and then settle for something that I really wanted to do. My parents were behind me and beside me, but they never pushed me to do things too prematurely. They were supportive, but not demanding. They were never in my face, which was great as well as rare in terms of many parents these days.

But my parents took that a step further. They made sure that I found something my heart was in, and then they urged me to do well at it. Do it 110 percent, they told me, as long as I enjoyed it. They felt that to do something, you should do it right and well — an investment of sorts on my part — and they would make a similar investment.

Whether it was driving me to weekend swim meets or to a soccer game or the ice skating rink, it was a huge investment on the part of my parents — an investment of time and money, which was so important to my success. The fact that they were willing to give of themselves so much meant I was exposed to all kinds of different things in the mainstream, which helped me find my niche.

That becomes particularly important for a hearing-impaired child. Not being exposed to different things means not being part of a team or an activity that you are good at and gives you pleasure. For me, athletics and particularly swimming was something that gave me confidence. The attitude of my parents was to make sure my heart was in it and then to put me in the right program.

❧

Academics was intense in high school. At Jesuit, there were no Mickey Mouse classes and no breaks. You had to have the grades, or you didn't last. Basically, I was competing against others who were strong students — and not handicapped — so I just had to adapt and do the best that I could.

Days were busy. Typical was to be at the pool club early for a workout from 6:00 A.M. to 7:15 A.M. School was less than a mile from the club, so I'd get there by 8:30 A.M. and have classes to around 2 P.M. before heading back to the pool for practice from 2:30 to 4:30 or 5:00. Then it was home for dinner, studying 'til 9:00 or 9:30, before going to bed and doing it all over again the next day.

So that was the week. On Saturday mornings, I typically had a swim practice or a meet. Then I'd get home and had to finish up any homework before my parents would let me do anything else.

Sure, it was intense, but it was very supportive as well. First and foremost, my parents were always there for me, And when I had a problem in class, there were tutors to help me, provided I had the extra time. But that could be difficult at times because I was getting pressure from my swim coach who wanted me to train.

❧

In 1978, I went to the University of Southern California on an athletic scholarship. I was heavily recruited in high school, having also received offers from U.C.L.A., Stanford, the University of California, the University of Tennessee and Vanderbilt, among others. Receiving all those offers was kind of overwhelming; I remember the stacks of letters from colleges.

I chose U.S.C. for its swimming program, of course, but I went there as well for its learning skills development center that provides lots of counseling for students, particularly those with special needs. It was a private university and class size was also much smaller than those of some of the other schools I considered. I just felt comfortable there.

I wouldn't say college was any easier. I think of it as more of a continuum of the structure I learned to keep in high school: My days were pretty tightly scheduled. I would tell myself, "these two hours are for training; these two for class, another 1.5 for study and some other time for eating or whatever." You just get to it; otherwise, things just don't get done. When the pressure is on, you respond and you need structure to do it; it's that simple.

As a scholarship athlete, I didn't exactly have a "normal" student life. Swimming was my focus and top priority. Class schedules were different from high school, because you could make the academics fit your schedule. But like I said, it was more or less the same, with two workouts a day and competition in the winter and spring semesters.

I majored in psychology, with a minor in business and marketing. Graduating took five years instead of the usual four because of the extra demands of swimming and the Olympic year of 1980. Those were the Moscow Olympics, which the U.S. Team boycotted as part of President Carter's protest against the Russian invasion of Afghanistan. Before the United States chose not to compete, I had to train strenuously to make the team. To help, I took a minimum number of courses — 13 units per semester, instead of the usual 16 or 18.

I made the 1980 Olympic team, but instead of going to Moscow, we went to Hawaii to train and compete. It was quite a year for me: I was in the top 10 in the world in three events, the 400 freestyle, the 200 fly and the 400 intermediate medley. At the Olympic Trials that year I had to swim finals for the 400 IM, as it's known, and the 200 fly on the same day, in fact only 1.5 hours apart. At the time, the 200 fly was my best event and I was hoping to make a run at the world record in the final. But I didn't swim well in that event, didn't get the world record and didn't even make the team in that event. It was a big disappointment.

By the time I reached my teens, I tried to engineer the fact that I was deaf and turn it to an advantage. You'll find that with people who have disabilities; their other senses increase: It's taking a disadvantage, tossing it aside and "going for it." And it's as much as establishing a "belief system" versus a "disbelief system" and giving yourself the ability to take things to the next level and beyond. For a deaf person, it can be learning to read lips or just blocking out the background noise so you can focus; there are a lot of ways that I, as a disabled person, can turn a situation into an advantage

❧

I've heard people say they're jealous of me because when I'm in a loud place, all I have to do is turn down my hearing aid and the noise doesn't bother me. But a lot of achievement really depends on your environment — I was lucky to have a coach who was a disciplinarian, older brothers and sisters who were overachievers, and supportive parents who let me channel my energies into positive things. That was so important.

I have two siblings, both of whom are considerably older. My brother, John, now an osteopathic doctor in Hawaii, is ten-and-a-half years older than me; and my sister, Joanne, a teacher in California who graduated from Stanford with a 4.0 grade point average and has a master's degree in education, is nine years older.

Sure, there was a generation gap when I was young, but both John and Joanne were good role models for me. My sister was a kind of second mom to me when I was really young — baby-sitting and teaching when our parents weren't around. And my brother was always there to play sports with me; he was a real "big bro." Of course, they were in high school when I was 7 or 8 and off in medical or graduate school when I was in high school and got into swimming big time. But they got to some of the big meets, when they could, and of course were at the Olympics, with my parents, in 1984.

❧

During my summer breaks in college, I'd always go home to Sacramento and train with my old club coach. I'd do that for eight weeks or so, before going to the National Championships, and depending on whether I qualified, the World Championships or the Pan American Games, each of which is held, like the Olympics, every four years. Add to that the international duel meets, particularly before and after the Olympics, and my opportunity to travel, for a time, was really quite extensive.

I've been fortunate to go to places like Bucharest, Romania, for the World Championships for the Deaf in 1977. I went to West Berlin for the '78 Worlds, to Guayaquil, Ecuador, for the '82 Worlds where we took the gold in the

4×200 relay, and to Brazil, Australia and Italy. Swimming has given me the opportunity to travel around the world, a kind of education in itself.

Swimming has also been the source of most of my close friendships. Of course, swimmers were my friends: We'd spend six hours a day training together and then go to meets on the weekends. Basically, they provided a strong network of friends who accepted me despite my hearing loss. Accepting it yourself is another matter and can be difficult, especially when you're in second and third grade and classmates are pulling at your hearing aids and you don't understand why.

But it's important that if you're deaf or hard of hearing, you just accept it. Kids taunting you is part of the process. Getting to the point of acceptance isn't a matter of waking up one day and having it happen. There are trials and tribulations along the way; with me, there were days when I didn't want to go to speech therapy. But I went anyway, which was good for me, whether I realized it or not back then. Dealing with things the best way you can is so important, along with a solid support network. Those without that support are the ones who struggle.

There was never a question on the part of my parents that they'd go the "oral" route and teach me to speak. After all, 98 percent of the population speak, and if you're going to adapt to the real world, why limit yourself to the 2 percent who aren't speakers? It sounds limiting to me.

I had an interesting experience when I went to Romania in 1977 for the World Championships for the Deaf. I saw it as an opportunity to swim, travel and see a bit of the other side of deaf life — the "signers." It was really eye-opening to me, because the signers wanted me to be one of the them — that is sign, instead of speak. I didn't grow up with sign language, so I had to learn the rudiments of it pretty quickly over there to get by and communicate.

On one hand, the signers liked me because I was a great athlete — I was a big dog in a little puddle and won 10 gold medals, setting 10 (deaf) world records in the process. On the other hand, some saw me as a phony, as someone who didn't sign exclusively and therefore, wasn't one of them.

I think the signers saw this as an event bringing kids together from all over the world, a bond of being hearing impaired or deaf, before going home and being a part of the minority again. I was kind of like a Disney World character to them. I certainly didn't feel that way and I remember there were three or four other athletes in the same situation — oral people who didn't know any sign language.

I just never felt any particular pull to joining the signers, to becoming "one of them." I was the only hearing-impaired student in my high school, but I never felt a need to join the signers, in part, because I just wasn't around other signers.

So those World Games were the first time I was ever around large numbers of other deaf people, and frankly, the rift or controversy over my not being a signer made it confusing. It even got to the point where some of the athletes and the officials of other countries looked at me as somebody who wasn't really deaf. Officials of a number of countries actually got together and singled me out —filing a protest, actually making me take a hearing test. There was a lot of backlash and a lot of politics going on there. So, I took the test and the results matched the ones I had submitted on my entry form. I wasn't "a cheat" after all.

&

Not fitting in with the signers doesn't mean I escape from fulfilling my sense of community responsibility. Winning an Olympic gold medal affords a rare opportunity to have a positive influence on a large segment of the population who need that kind of support. And I take it seriously; I don't laugh at it. I think I've attended so many functions, in which I passed around my gold medal, that the ribbon has seen better days. I guess I'll have to take it to the dry cleaner, sooner or later.

I don't limit the functions I attend to those aiding people with disabilities. I'm involved with a Southern California–based program called "People Reaching Out," in which I speak to people about the dangers of drugs. About once a month, I spend a day going to three or four schools in the area and talking to kids about some of the things I learned through swimming and as a handicapped person.

I tell them about setting goals and going after those goals with hard work. They are lessons that students can learn from and adapt to their own lives. Today's youth need some kind of focus other than aiming for a career in pro sports. I tell them that it's great to have a goal of making the NFL or the NBA, but that the odds of getting there are not good. You stand a better chance of winning the lottery than making it as a pro basketball player.

The way I see it, I'm in a unique position to tell them that: I was just an average kid who did something out of the ordinary because it was something I loved to do and I was good at it. It's rewarding for me, and if I can influence just one or two kids in a positive way, then it's worth the effort.

People always express a real curiosity about the Olympics. They want to know what drove me to get there and what it was like winning a gold medal. Of course, if I'd won a silver medal and not the gold, there wouldn't be any curiosity at all; people would want to know, "How come I didn't get the gold?" Unfortunately, that's an attitude that pervades our society — "either you win everything, or you're a loser."

I tell people that getting there took constant effort, day in and day out. Training and competing at a high level meant I was tired all the time, but I had to carry on to make it. If you fall, you have to get right back up and do it again. I also say that the really hard part of training was the first part — getting up at 5 A.M. and jumping in the pool. A lot of it came down to attitude: Once I got there and got in, it wasn't so bad.

Was winning the gold medal my proudest accomplishment? Yes, but I like to put it up there with graduating from college without debt and winning my first national title, in 1978. I remember everything about that first title: It was in the 400 freestyle and going into the event, I was seeded 27th out of 30 entrants. Going into the event, I had never broken four minutes, but then I qualified for the final with a 3:58.5.

The field for the final was unreal: the entire U.S. Olympic team from the 1976 Games, including the gold and silver medalists, Brian Goodell and Tim Shaw. I was in lane one, next to Goodell, who was also the world record holder at the time. I swam well, lopping another four seconds off my time and won the race, dropping in a year, from 4:03 to 3:54. Suddenly, everyone was asking, "Who is this guy?" You remember those things.

I look back and surprise myself: How did I do all those laps and stay so focused? Fortunately, I burned out at the right time, which was after the '84 Olympics. It was a natural progression and the best thing any athlete could ask for in terns of ending a career. Yes, I won the gold, but at the same time, I was sad at leaving my sport and losing that intensity of focus. Today, I have a different kind of focus: It's on nine or ten things at once, as opposed to one or two. But I was lucky to have been there. It taught me a lot.

Carolyn Ginsburg

NEW YORK, NEW YORK

Carolyn Ginsburg is a brand executive at a Fortune 500 consumer pack-aged goods company. A native of Long Island, New York, she is a graduate of Northwestern University and the Columbia University Graduate School of Business. She is a former fundraiser at the League for the Hard of Hearing in New York City.

I was born two months early — doctors believe this premature birth was the cause of my hearing loss. There is no trace of hearing impairment in my family, so I guess they're probably right.

My hearing loss was officially diagnosed in kindergarten when I started at the public school down the street from my house. At the beginning of the school year, all students were required to take the hearing screening test at the nurse's office.

I remember the day well. My classmates and I lined up outside the heath office waiting for our turn. I watched my friends go before me as they put on the headphones and tapped the pencil on the desk as instructed to indicate that they heard a sound. When it was my turn, I remember thinking, "Hey, how come I can't hear anything?" Realizing that all my classmates were watching me take my turn, I didn't want to look funny. So, I started hitting the pencil on the desk at different intervals to appear as if I heard something. The nurse asked me to stay back and talk to her once she was done with the other students. It was as if the big secret was found out, only now it had a name: deafness.

33

Prior to that, my parents thought I mispronounced words a lot, but they never associated it with hearing loss. Because I was a premature baby, my parents were told they had no reason to be concerned if there was any slowness on my part because I'd be caught up by the age of five. But my mother suspected something, and not long ago, she told me a "telling" story of the time when I was an infant and she took me to visit her good friend and daughter. While visiting this family, my mom asked her good friend's professional and experienced nanny if she thought I could hear normally. The nanny did a primitive hearing test by clapping her hands over my head. Whereas any hearing child would have been startled at the sound, I had no response. And yet there were no significant signs of my hearing impairment until I was tested in school as having a moderate loss.

My parents described me as a quiet baby who never made too much noise. They said I would lie in my crib for hours, doze and play by myself. Maybe I was quiet because I wasn't hearing the noises in the house, but my early memories of not hearing well do not really start until nursery school. I went to a neighborhood nursery school with my parents' friends' children my age, some of whom I am still friendly with today. My memory of hearing loss that stands out most was during story time of day when we would gather 'round the teacher who would read us a story. I vaguely remember realizing that if I sat close to the teacher I could hear her, but if I sat farther away on my nap blanket, I wouldn't hear. But unfortunately, as a youngster, I didn't know this was something I should tell the adults, nor was it an awareness I even knew how to express.

I grew up with two sisters, one of whom is 18 months older, and the other, three years younger. Neither sister developed a hearing loss — I was the only one. My sisters and I knew there was something different about me — that I had different needs than they did in terms of hearing.

Because I had a hard time hearing our family's only TV at the normal volume, we came up with a rule: I would watch one TV show at my sisters' preferred volume, which was so low I had to sit right next to the TV and then I would get to watch the next TV show at my volume. Watching at my volume was quite loud, and they would tell me how it would hurt their ears. (I didn't have a TV with captioning until my mid-20s). My mother also tells me of the several times she would call my name from another room or when I wasn't facing her, and I wouldn't respond. But, it took the elementary school hearing test to finally give what I had a name and a semicure — hearing aids.

Carolyn Ginsburg

In the beginning of first grade, I finally got my first hearing aid after taking many trips from our home in the Long Island suburbs into New York City with my mother for second opinions, and then appointments with the audiologist. I remember hating how much time it took to do all the doctor appointments and how I would get nauseous in the car while sitting in traffic.

The first night wearing my hearing aid at home, I remember we were eating dinner on the porch. I was startled by the loud noise above and had to ask what I was hearing. My parents were so surprised and they told me it was an airplane passing above on its way to La Guardia Airport. I couldn't believe airplanes could make such a loud sound! As the days progressed, I discovered new sounds I had never heard before and redefined old sounds that I started hearing with more clarity. I also was able to hear on the phone better and in the classroom, too.

Most of the children I have met through the League for the Hard of Hearing as well as my friends who are hard of hearing or deaf have had to take many years of speech therapy. I was fortunate enough to have been able to develop language skills on my own, which was probably because I must have had enough hearing to develop language during the critical two to four year old age group. However, I do remember my mother frequently correcting my pronunciation and at times she was frustrated with me when I didn't say something correctly.

When I was in fifth and sixth grade, my parents took me for speech therapy with a wonderfully dedicated speech therapist. She taught me my strengths and how to manage my weaknesses — like hearing and articulating consonants (S, T, B, F in particular) — and hearing and saying the beginning and ending of words clearly. I never liked going to speech therapy, but it was just something I had to do.

By the time I entered seventh grade, the school system provided me with an itinerant teacher — an educational specialist in hearing loss. She had two roles: first, to help me manage any issues that came up because of my hearing loss and to help me talk to my teachers, and second, help me develop stronger and better communication skills such as speech reading and the ability to hear better in noisy situations.

On the one hand, I was grateful to have her help. I finally had a cushion, someone to help buffer some of the stress of going to a competitive and academically challenging public school with a hearing loss. On the other hand, I hated being singled out, being different and having to deal with this deficiency. I think I felt this way intensely because I didn't have friends who were hearing impaired or any role models; few even knew I had a hearing loss, let alone wore hearing aids. So I did everything I could to hide my hearing loss. I would wear my hair long to cover my hearing aids. I would go to all lengths to avoid having to tell someone I wasn't hearing them, and worst was I would pretend that I was hearing everything in class. This went on for many years throughout middle school and high school.

But, when I got to Northwestern University in Chicago, my strategy was no longer working. College was real stuff. The hearing loss really became a liability and I could no longer "fake it" as I had done as a youngster. Classes were large, the course work was challenging, and many professors graded on class participation, which was a terrifying thing for a student with a hearing loss who is trying to follow classroom discussions. For the first time, I was really put to the test of having to face my hearing loss and tell my professors and my classmates. But I was often terrified to do this because I was afraid to admit there was something different about me, that I needed assistance.

Somehow I got by in college. I didn't yet know about the FM [assistive listening] unit that can be used with my hearing aids to hear better in the classroom. Nor did I know about CART, Computer-Aided Real Time captioning or oral interpreters. Then again, the option of using a sign language interpreter wouldn't have been applicable to me because I didn't know sign language growing up. (I know it now, thanks to the two years of classes I took in my mid–20s.) So, being a student at times was quite overwhelming and lonely as well because the hearing loss created a barrier between the rich classroom learning experience and my ability to participate.

The hearing loss also presented challenges with basic student life on campus. The big focus in college was also the social life — going to loud, noisy, dark parties and bars, as well as doing things in big groups. It was in those situations that I often wished I wasn't hearing impaired. At times, socializing was more work than fun as I tried to follow conversations with blasting loud music in dark rooms. But since I could communicate very well one-on-one, I thrived in developing close friendships in the dorm, through my classes and extracurricular activities. I did everything I could to put myself in comfortable communication settings.

∽

I majored in art history and took a lot of art classes at Northwestern. After graduation, I knew I wanted to do something in the creative field. So with that, and my passion for architecture, I worked as a design assistant at an interior design and architecture firm in New York City for three years.

It was then that, I found out about the League for the Hard of Hearing and had my first chance to meet my first friend with hearing loss. Her name was Alison, and we both enjoyed sharing our experiences with hearing loss and developed a friendship beyond hearing loss.

Also, Alison and I really became eager to meet other hearing impaired professionals in New York. We started a networking group called the LINK which met once or twice a month, for meetings and outings. I had a great time meeting many different types of hearing-impaired people who were oral communicators.

To this very day, I still have some close friendships that were established from this group, and we still get together from time to time. In fact I found that I enjoyed the connection to hearing impairment and the League so much that I decided to find out if I could work there full-time. When an exciting opportunity came up to fundraise for the League, I jumped on it and wound up spending four years there. During that time, I helped the League raise money through organizing special events, direct mail campaigns and individual solicitations.

∽

In time, I knew I wanted to pursue a graduate degree. Although I was always very ambitious and studious, I didn't think I could do it because I lacked the motivation to repeat the frustrations and isolation I felt in the classroom experience in undergrad.

Fortunately, by working at the League, I learned about many ways to improve my educational experience. So armed finally with the confidence to pursue my dream and go back to graduate school and earn an MBA, I took the plunge. Studied for the GMATs, wrote my applications and was awarded admission to Columbia University's Graduate School of Business.

This time, I wanted to do things differently. And boy, oh boy, were things different! Six months before school started, I met with the Office for Students with Disabilities and the administrators of the business school. We discussed what types of accommodations I needed, and after clearly explaining my needs, they willingly supported me. To make school easier, I purchased my first FM unit, which all my professors wore.

Also for each class, I had CART provided. With CART a skilled courtroom stenographer would come to each of my classes and would type verbatim what was said in the classroom discussions. The text would appear on the computer laptop screen next to me, and for the first time ever, I was able to follow discussions and even participate! It helped make business school, while very challenging, a rewarding experience.

While at Columbia, I decided to take a break from working in the hearing impaired field and non-profit world, and try something new. So, I decided to pursue a career in marketing and management at a large Fortune 500 consumer products company, where I've been working for almost three years and really enjoying it. The MBA prepared me well to do this job, yet, there's a ton of on the job learning and training classes. I guess it's true that hearing loss is for life until they invent a pill to eradicate the problem.

But having said that, I still have to manage my hearing loss at work on a daily basis. That's because my job is extremely communication-intensive. I attend meetings of all sizes, ranging from four to more than 20 people, all day long. I do as much as I can to advocate for myself: I try to use my FM as much as possible, and when I can, I schedule a CART reporter to attend my training classes. Sometimes I wish I didn't have to deal with the hearing loss on top of having a challenging and stressful job, but on the other hand, there are days when my co-workers are interestingly envious that I can turn my hearing aids off and concentrate on my work at my desk in silence. As much as I can, I try to focus on the positive things about being hearing impaired.

For me, being hearing impaired is a unique experience. I'm still amazed that by the flip of an on-switch I can be in the hearing world as a hard of hearing person, or I can flip the off-switch and be in the non-hearing or deaf world. I feel lucky and fortunate to have this choice.

Evelyn Glennie

CAMBRIDGESHIRE, UNITED KINGDOM

"The program promised concerto," started the concert review in The Philadelphia Inquirer, *"but the Philadelphia Orchestra audience got theater, magic, tumult and romance."* What it got was Evelyn Glennie, the world's first full-time, solo percussionist. That the Scottish-born Glennie, is profoundly deaf is not mentioned, until well into the review, is typical. That it goes on to give a laudatory report of Glennie's performance — "the soloist creates clouds of sound, a pulse as vital as heartbeats and a theatrical scene that evokes the romance of Sir Walter Scott," — is typical, too. Indeed, Glennie's performance is a wonder, bridging the gap between musical brilliance, athleticism and performance art. Shoeless, she flies from instrument to instrument, creating a crescendo of sound that is hard to forget.

A graduate of the Royal Academy of Music in London, Glennie performs with many of the world's greatest orchestras and conductors, often premiering new pieces written especially for her. A Grammy Award–winner for her recording of Bartok's Sonata for Two Pianos and Percussion with Sir Georg Solti, Murray Perahia and David Corkhill, she is the recipient of several honorary doctorates and has won many awards and honors, including an Officer of the British Empire.

Glennie would rather discuss music than her deafness. She has collaborated with indigenous musicians throughout Britain, Ireland, India and Venezuela, and has performed with the gamelan orchestras in Indonesia and samba bands in Brazil. When away from her hectic schedule — she gives more than 100 performances a year — Glennie enjoys playing the great highland bagpipes, painting, and collecting antiques as well as old and new musical instruments.

❧

Most musicians really use a sense of touch; many musicians, of course, translate that sense of touch into what's coming through their ears. Although I can't do that to the extent the others can, the only difference with me is that I can use my body as a resonating chamber.

Not long ago, a group of 40 students from the American School for the Deaf in Hartford came to watch my rehearsal. They came up on stage and I asked them, "How many of you play a musical instrument?" None did. "Why?," I asked them. "We can't hear it," they said.

And so I played something on the marimba and asked if they could experience the sound. "Yes," several said.

"So how many of you have been to a concert?" I asked.

None had. "Why?" I asked. "We can't hear the music," they said.

But after they attended the rehearsal, suddenly 90 percent of them wanted tickets to attend the regular concert.

Evelyn Glennie

What I was really trying to do was direct my statements to the teachers of the students. That's because many times the teachers are the ones who assume these people can't hear in conventional ways. Music is all about sound — it's creating sound — so how on earth can deafness, which in a blank statement means silence, correspond with music, which is all about sound?

Those American School for the Deaf students really got to feeling and experiencing with all the subtle sounds — it wasn't just loud or soft — and I could really see them begin to cue their bodies to the various sensations. It was a very, very interesting experience and it only lasted about 20 minutes. So, I really hope that the teachers there think a little bit more from now on about bringing music to these students. There are schools throughout the U.K. where young deaf kids have the opportunity to learn a musical instrument in the same way that a mainstreamed high school student would. Some kids aren't going to go for it, but some students will, because the musical seed will be there, as it was with me.

The disturbing thing to me at that rehearsal is that none of those kids played anything because they just weren't given the opportunity. At the same time, that rehearsal gave them the chance to experience a good orchestra right on their doorstep. Many kids don't get that opportunity at all. The sensations, expressions and comments of these students from the American School showed that they know how to think for themselves. Often, for deaf kids, too much thinking is done for them.

Music represents life. A particular piece of music may describe a real, fictional or abstract scene from almost any area of human experience or imagination. It is the musician's job to paint a picture that communicates to the audience the scene the composer is trying to describe.

I hope that the audience will be stimulated by what I have to say through the language of music and will therefore leave the concert hall feeling entertained. If the audience is instead only wondering how a deaf musician can play percussion, then I have failed as a musician. For this reason, my deafness isn't mentioned in any of the information supplied by my office to the press or concert promoters. Unfortunately, my deafness makes good headlines, and I have learned from childhood that if I refuse to discuss my deafness with the media, they will just make it up.

The several hundred articles and reviews written about me every year add up to a total of many thousands, but only a handful accurately describe my hearing impairment. More than 90 percent are so inaccurate that it would seem impossible that I could be a musician.

Music heightens my senses. There are all kinds of things that happen in performance that do not happen even in a practice room. Every hall, every orchestra and every instrument is different. I really feel that most musicians, even if they're not aware of it, really do use their senses in a heightened way. As a musician, your whole visual sense and sense of touch are always a lot more extreme in performance, which is why I often practice away from my instruments, because then, I can imagine how I'm to be in concert. That way, I imagine the sounds I want to create from my instruments. Everything I imagine is perfect, which is really important, so I'm not hindered by the actual mechanical points of playing the instruments.

Doing that, I'm only thinking about the musical statement I want to make. To me, that's the really important thing to playing well. At the end of the day, the audience doesn't care if you're a percussionist or play the clarinet or the violin — the majority of the audience don't necessarily know the difference between a good and a very good percussionist in much the same way that I don't know the difference between a good and a very good organist. In that situation, all I really know is that if somebody affects me, then that's great. That's the important thing.

It's particularly important for parents of hearing impaired children to let their children explore their interests. Another question I asked of the group of American School students who visited was how many of them had ever been next to a double bass? No one. Or a trombone? Same answer. So, I challenged them some more, asking, "How do you know that you can't play those instruments?" And, "How do you know that the chemistry between you and those instruments isn't going to be good?"

I would want to expose them to as many different experiences in life, from concerts of folk music to Latin music and classical concerts. And, I'd want to take them to an art gallery and see whether they love to create things through paints or pencils. And take them to the theater or a sports event, or anything. These are the sorts of things you'd normally be doing anyway, provided you had the facilities and resources nearby.

Deafness is poorly understood in general. There is a common misconception that deaf people live in a world of silence. To understand the nature of deafness, you first have to understand the nature of hearing.

Hearing is basically a specialized form of touch. Sound is simply vibrating air that the ear picks up and converts to electrical signals that are then interpreted by the brain. The sense of hearing is not the only sense that can do this, touch can do this, too.

If you are standing by the road and a large truck goes by, do you hear or feel the vibration? The answer is both. With very low frequency vibration, the ear starts becoming inefficient and the rest of the body's sense of touch starts to take over. For some reason we tend to make a distinction between hearing a sound and feeling a vibration, in reality they are the same thing.

It is interesting to note that in the Italian language this distinction does not exist. The verb "sentire" means to hear and the same verb in the reflexive form "sentirsi" means to feel. Deafness does not mean that you can't hear, only that there is something wrong with the ears. Even someone who is totally deaf can still hear and feel sounds.

If we can all feel low frequency vibrations why can't we feel higher vibrations? It is my belief that we can; it's just that as the frequency gets higher and our ears become more efficient they drown out the more subtle sense of "feeling" the vibrations.

I spent a lot of time when I was young, with the help of Ron Forbes, my percussion teacher at school, refining my ability to detect vibrations. I would stand with my hands against the classroom wall, while Ron played notes on the timpani, which produce a lot of vibrations.

Eventually, I managed to distinguish the rough pitch of notes by associating where on my body I felt the sound with the sense of perfect pitch I had before losing my hearing. The low sounds I feel mainly in my legs and feet and high sounds might be particular places on my face, neck and chest.

Growing up with my parents and two brothers in a farm outside Aberdeen, Scotland, I was never treated as a special case. Part of the reason was that my parents didn't know how to treat me any differently, but also because life just went on as normally as it did after I lost my hearing. Why should it suddenly change when, at age 12, I lost my hearing? What was so important about my upbringing was how normal it all was; it was all very unfussy, which is very much a trait of Scottish people, who do not typically make a big deal of things and do not turn someone into a special case. Everybody just acted normal, which was the best thing that could have happened. Looking back, I had a good upbringing.

Obviously though, there had to be something more — the inner seed and the inner desire and focus of the ideas I was after, and that has to come from me. That goes for anyone. Add to my case, a lot of support from my parents, which often involved ushering me to this place and that place for rehearsals, and putting up with all the practice. Yes, they were very supportive.

And, in my case, there was something else; musically, my biggest challenge has been the percussion repertoire, so I'm thankful to a lot of the music clubs throughout the U.K. and further afield for giving me the opportunity early in my career to put on a percussion recital, which, in itself, is very unusual.

So, where does the deafness fit in? In my case, it has frankly always been secondary; it's just very much a part of me, in the same way that I have brown hair. To me, it's just another challenge to being a good musician.

I'm not totally deaf. I'm profoundly deaf, which covers a wide range of symptoms, although it is commonly taken to mean that the quality of the sound heard is not sufficient to be able to understand the spoken word from sound alone. With no other sound interfering, I can usually hear someone speaking although I cannot understand them without the additional input of lipreading. In my case, the amount of volume is reduced compared with normal hearing but more importantly the quality of the sound is very poor.

For instance, when a telephone rings, I hear a kind of crackle. However, it's a distinctive type of crackle that I associate with a phone, so I know when it rings. This is basically the same as how people with regular hearing detect a phone; it has a distinctive type of ring that most people associate with a phone. My husband and I, in fact, can, communicate over the phone. I do most of the talking, but we have a few words that he can communicate by hitting the transmitter with a pen, which I hear as clicks. We have a code that depends on the number of hits or the rhythm that I can use to communicate a handful of words.

What does it take to be a good musician? It varies. For me, knowing what I want to do musically and within the music business is important. I knew from the age of 15 that I wanted to be a percussion soloist, and that was that. Obviously, that involves being the best musician you want to be, which takes practice and literally playing as much as you can and in as many different situations as you can. And it involves — at least in the beginning — taking jobs and accepting concert dates, whether you're paid for it or not. Kind of "paying your dues," in a way. And that applies to any job or situation.

It's also important to have goals — both short- and long-term. I have goals, both musically and in the music business itself. That's a big distinction, because one of the things the musicologists don't teach you is about the actual business of being a musician, because playing your instrument is only part of it all.

It also involves issues like figuring out the logistics of getting the equipment from point A to point B, which for a percussionist is all very important. Had I been a violinist or played the clarinet, I wouldn't have to deal with any of those issues and I might have had some extra hours in the week to do something else. You literally have to keep playing and practicing, just to be prepared; and you have to sometimes say "yes" to playing a piece you don't know too well. In that case, you just learn it.

But it takes more than just hard work to be a success. Nowadays, there are so many youngsters who have a chance to play an instrument, so there are lots of people who can play and play well. You may have two extremely good percussionists, for instance, but only one who will create a statement.

In music today, it really is imagination that is probably the biggest ingredient of all that sets a person apart. I know that many of the pieces I play can be played by countless people; it's the imagination of putting your own stamp on a piece that is something you can either do or you can't. Sometimes, people can do that very quickly and the statement becomes predictable, so you lose the spark. Other times, it can take people a long time to find their "voice," but when it comes, it's pretty amazing. And sometimes, people can find it and create different sparks in each performance.

I started percussion at the age of 12. It started from curiosity, like any kid who has a fancy for something. You just have these phases of interest — like somebody who wants to be the greatest astronaut or fireman or musician — and I went through it like anyone else. I somehow knew that I needed music in my life; music wasn't part of our household so much, although my parents liked and listened to Scottish traditional music. It was really just something I knew I liked. That's why I feel it's important to present music to young people in schools, where you hope that, like me, a seed might be planted.

With my parents, certainly — and it happened with both percussion and piano — I had to lobby a bit, that is ask them over a period of several months for lessons. With the piano lessons, in particular, it took awhile, because they just assumed this was all a passing fancy and they wanted to be sure that I was really serious about it. That, in turn, made it easier for them to accept something as unusual as percussion; because I liked piano, they more readily accepted the percussion. Yes, it was not an ordinary musical interest, but my parents knew I was serious; they knew to stand back and watch that interest grow at its own pace.

I was one of two deaf students of the 1,300 who attended my comprehensive school. We were a kind of a revelation to the teaching staff; they really didn't know how to deal with us or what to do. The result is they didn't make too many allowances, which, in hindsight, I regard as an advantage. In most cases, that worked pretty well, and the school had a visiting tutor for Michael, the other deaf student, and me. That was a tremendous help because the tutor specialized in working with deaf people.

So, in fact, I do regard myself as quite lucky as far as what the school provided because it meant that I could have the services I wanted. The situation was right for my needs at the time, because I wanted to be very independent. Of course, when you're wearing hearing aids as a teenager, I found that I was very conscious of them; I was sure to keep my hair over my ears to hide them. I consider it, perhaps, natural to be that way as a teenager; at the time, you're going through all sorts of changes and having to wear hearing aids, I found, was very disturbing.

Typically, I didn't tell people that I wore hearing aids, that is, until some mishap, like batteries going flat, which could make you suddenly very isolated. It could be disturbing until friends would rally 'round and help out. I just happen to have had a really good bunch of friends, who just accepted me and everyone else as they were.

In hindsight, I realize that concept of friendship — the importance of having really good friends — extends to everybody. Certainly, a musician's life is up and down, up and down. You have a lot of emotional changes within minutes sometimes. For instance, you wake up all bright and breezy one morning and open the newspaper to find a bad review; you're miserable for the rest of the day. Or it could be that you get extremely nervous before a performance, meaning there's all this extra trauma to go through that partners, friends and colleagues have to deal with as well. The point is that everybody needs a strong network of support.

Going to secondary school with a hearing impairment was hard, but mostly because of me and not the disability. In other words, I made the deafness my problem; I was just so conscious of being deaf. It was also the transition I went through in losing my hearing at a time when I thought that the answer to proper hearing was turning up the volume. But socially, it wasn't too much of a problem; my network of friends and my teachers were supportive and accommodating. As I said, it was something that I had to deal with myself.

Indeed, leaving home to attend the Royal Academy in London wasn't difficult. By that time, I had gotten a grip on what I wanted to do — and I was very singular-minded and very determined and independent in my goals. I knew the goal I was after — and there was no social life whatsoever. I just worked and worked and worked for three years, did well and then I left.

❧

Today, I feel a strong desire to give back and contribute to the community. At the moment, I do what I can, but because all my energies and efforts and thinking have gone into my full-time solo percussion career — and I'm the only one in the world — it's hard to find the time. I not only have to find the pieces, but I have to learn and get a platform for them. And if you think of the amount of things attached to a career in music — it's the recording, the videos and the writing, as well — you start to get an idea of where the time goes. But I do find the time for community things. I'm a patron of more than 80 charities and I actually participate in a handful of them.

But where I really feel I'm contributing is through my concerts themselves. One of the things that always strikes me about them is the huge variety of people who attend. It's a different audience to the usual subscribers — and there are always lots of young people there, from infants and children to grandmas and grandpas, and from music critics and those who are knowledgeable about music to the curious and people who just like drums.

So, in fact, I'm targeting many people in a normal performance. Also, things like the Internet mean the beginnings of a virtual master class in percussion, which is another important step to take, because it's becoming increasingly difficult for me to actually make appearances in schools and colleges. I used to do a lot of that, but because of time constraints and trying to keep everything going at the moment, I find it more and more difficult to spread myself.

You have to remember that a lot of years go by before you build a base. I'm in my 30s, but I'm still considered a "young musician." In the music business, you have prodigies and teen musicians, and I'm still lumped into the "young musician" category, which means I have to go with the flow. I feel it's going to be another decade or so — when I have more experience at performance and at delivery — before I'm really ready to do significant in the community, in addition to my performances. Basically, it boils down to timing and having to feel right. At the moment, it doesn't feel right for me to go or be everywhere at once.

Do deaf people have to work harder to be successful? I do, but for as long as I can remember, I've been a busybody who has to be doing things. It's very difficult for me to just sit and watch television or something. And I always feel guilty going on holiday or just stopping my work, although I'm beginning to experiment a bit more with time and trying to control it more efficiently without always feeling I have to be on the go.

I give about 120 concerts a year. That's a lot for any musician, considering I travel with at least a ton of equipment, all of which needs to be organized very meticulously. On top of that, the whole development of repertoire is a huge area that can take years to fulfill; one piece can take maybe three or four years before it's actually completed. Elsewhere, I have a whole education series that's suitable for classroom music teachers and another for writing music for television and radio. All are important sidelines, which I'm trying to develop. Add all the practice and preparation and it's just natural to go along at this pace.

I don't sign, and, in fact, know only a few basic pieces of British sign language. It's difficult for me to take a position on the oral versus signing controversy, because I'm a deafened person — and not somebody who was born deaf. For me, this is where the controversy stops. All I can say is that I'm a believer in both together, hand-in-hand. I'm not a believer in signing only, but I am a believer in oral only. At the same time, I'm a believer in the two coming together.

That is something I find quite interesting about the group of deaf students I mentioned before, the ones who attended my rehearsal: some of them could speak really well and were absolutely confident, whereas others didn't speak at all, and still others spoke and signed. I feel if I knew of someone who had lost their hearing like me, I'd want them to keep their oral skills. As a musician, I feel it is absolutely vital that I sing what I'm producing, which would have been totally lost had I not been oral. After all, I'm a sound creator.

As in the U.S., there is a war in Britain between the signers and the oralists at the moment. Perhaps I can put it in perspective: I have deaf friends who are musicians — among them, people I would say are very good amateurs. And I have one deaf friend, a viola player, in the London Symphony Orchestra, who lost her hearing when she was 15 or 16. All of these people speak well and with confidence, so much so that they have confidence enough to approach a stranger in the street for directions. Having that confidence, I think, is what it's about.

Taking that thought a step further, I think if you're going to sign only, then you had better be prepared that you will only to be able to communicate with other signers. It really is a language. So, you either use the common language — that is, you learn to speak, as opposed to sign only. It's the same way as learning spoken English — it's the common world language — and later learning German or French. I see sign language in the same way.

Everyone has some hearing, even if their loss is profound. In concert, I am typically accompanied by an orchestra, which features high sounds and broad sounds, as well as instruments that produce thin sounds and great big, round balloon sounds. Everyone in the audience is going to experience these sounds differently, and it's not just a case of "Can you hear that? ... yes or no?" The answers vary: It might be "I can" or rather "I can get the impact of that sound, but once it deteriorates, I can't." Or it might be getting a few seconds of the fade, before it goes away completely, or even a harsh sound before mellowing out.

It isn't just a case of hearing it or not hearing it; that, I find, is so frustrating when, like I said before, I deal with reporters and reviewers, because they don't often understand that concept and they're transmitting that misunderstanding to the public.

Deafness is not a black and white issue and appreciating the subtleties of sound gets to the root of how every individual perceives things. For instance, in talking with female violin soloists, I find a lot of them love to wear dresses that reveal their shoulders, so they can actually feel the body of the violin on their bare skin. And they are hearing musicians.

One of the world's great violinists, Anne-Sophie Mutter of Germany, is known for that kind of dress, saying she needs it for the communication and that she really needs to feel the violin when she plays. In much the same way, I take my shoes off when I play, partly because the marimba and vibraphone I use are not height-adjustable, so I'm a better height without shoes, and partly because I have to travel from one station to another and have to be very quiet. But it's also to feel more connected with sound. To explain that is very difficult, because many people ask, "Is that how you hear?" Partly, but that's not the whole answer.

So, is hearing loss ever an advantage? In my situation, it's an advantage because it allows me to put my stamp on the interpretation of the music. I don't rely on recordings in order to know how a piece should go. Most people do, because it's a quick way to learn a piece. But I have to learn the full score and basically read it. So, everything I do is entirely mine, whether you like it or not, which I think in the long run, is a tremendous advantage because it gives me confidence in what I want to say. There are no rules at all.

I suppose it's a bit like the way I speak. I have a Scottish accent and it's never going to go away because that's what I heard as a youngster. Now, if I spend many years living in America, I'm not going to become Americanized through my accent because there isn't enough to pick up. It's the same with music; if you're not going to hear somebody else's interpretation, what do you have? You have what you have to give, your own interpretation. That's an advantage.

On the other hand, there are times when playing with orchestras that I'm just not hearing something. Quite often, the music comes off as just a barrage of sound. And sometimes, all I want is the flute or the trumpet, but I have all the other noise to get through. That can be frustrating and off-putting. In those situations, the problem usually comes down to the scoring; if it's scored for lots of brass and wind instruments and all you need is to hang on to the lead trumpet player, it can get a little confusing if something else is protruding. It's like being in a pub or at a big dinner table where it's crowded and you're trying to communicate. It's easier for deaf people in smaller, less noisy surroundings.

So far, I've covered the hearing of sounds and the feeling of vibrations. But, there is one other element to the equation: sight. We can also see items move and vibrate. If I see a drum head or cymbal vibrate or even see the leaves of a tree moving in the wind, then subconsciously, my brain creates a corresponding sound. A common and ill-informed question from interviewers is, "How can you be a musician when you can't hear what you're doing?" The answer is that I couldn't be a musician if I weren't able to hear. Another often-asked question is, "How do you hear what you are playing?"

The logical answer is, "How does anyone hear?" An electrical signal is generated in the ear and various bits of other information from our other senses are sent to the brain, which then processes the data to create a sound picture. The various processes involved in hearing a sound are very complex but we all do it subconsciously, so we group all these processes together and call it simply listening.

The same goes for me. Some of the processes or original information may be different from people with normal hearing, but to hear sound, all I do is listen. Frankly, I have no more of an idea of how I hear than anyone else.

Much of this discussion is heading toward areas of philosophy. Who can say that when two normally hearing people hear a sound, they hear the same sound? I would suggest that everyone's hearing is different. All we can say is that the sound picture built up by their brain is the same, so that outwardly, there is no difference. For me, as for everyone, I'm better at certain things with my hearing than I am with others. To compensate, I need to lip-read to understand speech, although my awareness of the acoustics in a concert venue is excellent. For instance, I will even sometimes describe an acoustic in terms of how thick the air feels.

My hearing impairment is something that bothers other people far more than it bothers me. There are a couple of inconveniences, but in general, it doesn't affect my life much. My deafness is no more important than the fact that I'm a 5'2" female, with brown eyes. Sure, I sometimes have to find solutions to problems related to my hearing and music, but so do all musicians.

Most of us know very little about hearing. Likewise, I don't know very much about deafness, and, what's more, I'm not particularly interested. I remember one occasion when I uncharacteristically became upset with a reporter for constantly asking questions only about my deafness. "If you want to know about deafness, you should interview an audiologist," I told him. "My specialty is music."

David James

Dr. David James is an Associate Professor of Mathematics at Howard University. A native of Chicago, he is a graduate of Shimer College and earned his doctorate in mathematics from the University of Chicago. He taught at Rutgers University, before joining the Howard faculty in 1979. A past member of the Board of Directors of the Alexander Graham Bell Association for the Deaf, James was a 1996 recipient of the National Council on Communicative Disorders (NCCD) Achievement Award. He, his wife Becky, and their two daughters live in the Capitol Hill section of Washington, D.C.

I was born in Chicago in 1950 and became deaf from meningitis in 1955. Since I was four and already speaking, I had a much easier time than a child born deaf. But I had to learn to speak by feel rather than by hearing myself, and to understand speech by using my residual hearing and reading lips. It took several years before I could do this to any reasonable degree. I also had to learn to walk all over again because I'd lost my inner-ear sense of balance along with my hearing.

When I recovered, my parents were told that I was too deaf to be able to get any benefit from hearing aids. They went ahead anyway, figuring it couldn't hurt. So I was fitted with a hearing aid and immediately tore it off; it was uncomfortable and I didn't want to wear it at all. Also, one of my playmates had a live-in grandfather with a hearing aid, so I already associated it with old people.

One day, my mother had me go out with her and bring my hearing aid. She took me to my playmate's house, and my friend and his parents were there. My mother asked me to show them my hearing aid, and they all made it clear that they admired it. Then we left and went to another set of neighbors, an older couple. There the same thing happened: They wanted me to show them my hearing aid and showed every sign of delight when I did. So it went, all the way down the block. Everyone wanted to see my hearing aid, and congratulated me on having it.

The experience made me realize I was still part of the community; people still wanted

David James

to communicate with me. I came to see the hearing aid as a bridge to my friends, a way through the barrier that had come down between us. After that I wanted to wear it. I went to regular kindergarten and it didn't work out very well. Probably nothing would have — I lost my hearing in the spring of 1955 and when I started kindergarten that fall I really wasn't able to understand any speech. I got through the year somehow but it was clear that something different would have to be done.

My state caseworker recommended that I be sent away to the state school for the deaf to learn sign because I was too deaf for anything else, for there to be any hope of speech. But my parents figured it was bad enough that I'd lost my hearing and that I shouldn't be sent away and lose my family, too. They found a deaf education specialist through Catholic Charities and, with her help, worked out a plan. I would start first grade at a Catholic day school for the deaf and begin learning to read there; as soon as my reading was good enough — as it turned out, by the beginning of the next semester — I'd be transferred to a mainstream school.

I remember liking the school for the deaf because it had a great jungle gym and they gave me an automatic pencil that I thought was really cool. But I don't really have any memories of interacting with the other children there, and if there was any signing — it was officially an oral school — it completely escaped my notice.

The less than ideal experience I'd had in kindergarten caused my parents to look for a different school for the second semester, and they found another parochial school that was much farther away but where the teachers had a much better attitude. I went there and it worked out well. The teachers were competent and sensible. They were very conscientious about facing me when they spoke and giving me supplementary reading. By this time, also, I'd begun to get the hang of reading lips and using my residual hearing, and was steadily getting better at understanding speech. It all worked out so well that I skipped a couple of grades.

I think it's just as well that my parents decided not to have me learn to sign. Learning to read was as much work for me as for most children, and I had to work equally hard, or harder, to learn to understand speech again. If I'd had to learn sign, it would have been at the expense of one or both of those things, simply by diverting time and effort from them.

As it was, my parents kept reading to me out loud, which was very helpful in developing my ability to use my residual hearing. Then, as soon as I was able to read at a reasonably fluent level, they started having me read out loud to my siblings. I'm the oldest of six children, and our parents put a lot of work into creating situations like that which encouraged me to talk to them and them to talk to me. For another example, when my brothers and sisters had homework questions my parents would always refer them to me as in "Go and ask David." I answered everything from the capital of Bolivia to the number of planets in the solar system, that kind of stuff. These things helped keep us engaged with each other and keep me part of the family.

I went to Chicago's St. Ignatius High School, a heavy-duty Jesuit school. There I was one of 30 students in a classroom, one of the 100 or more students each teacher saw every day, and I had to accept that the teachers were not going to remember that I was deaf or to say everything facing me.

And there was a more fundamental problem, a dilemma. If I tried to follow what the teacher said, I couldn't look down and take notes. If I did take notes, for example, copying what was written on the blackboard, that meant missing what the teacher was saying. Of course, I could hear nothing of what the other students were saying, although sometimes I could get the teacher's answer and figure out what the question had been. With all these inefficiencies, I had to work extremely hard for mediocre grades.

I still managed to learn a lot. It helped that several teachers, on their own or with a little prompting from my parents at parent-teacher conferences, came to understand that I heard very little of what they said in class and tried to work out more effective ways of interacting with me, such as directed supplementary readings. My mathematics and English teachers were particularly good at this, and I responded by doing very well in those subjects.

Toward the end of my time there, I was getting As in English and math and Cs in everything else. In the process I discovered, or learned, that I could write rather well and that mathematics was something I was distinctly interested in as well as good at.

There was another, less pleasant element to my experience in high school. The school drew its students from all over Chicago, and rather few of them were black in those days — I was one of six blacks in the 240 students who graduated in my year. I was also smaller than most of my classmates for the first two years or so, since I was two years younger than the usual age for my grade — I was 15 when I graduated. The 1960s were an era of racial tension, and I was small and deaf and black, so I had a tough time for a while.

Eventually, it was time to move on to college, and to figure out how to pay for it. One of the things my parents and I looked into was the Illinois state government's Division of Vocational Rehabilitation. The DVR counselor we spoke with suggested a school I had never heard of before, Gallaudet College in Washington. While I was abstractly intrigued by the concept of a college just for deaf people, I had absolutely no interest in going to such a place myself.

I had already found the school I wanted to go to, Shimer College, a small Great Books college in the cornfields of Mount Carroll, Illinois, about 130 miles west of Chicago. Happily, the DVR did not insist on Gallaudet and helped pay my way to Shimer. I was 16 years old when I started there. I enrolled as a regular student, but there were several other freshmen my age thanks to an early entrance program.

It was great. One of the reasons I picked it was that at such a small school — it had only 300 students — I wouldn't get lost in the crowd. I thought it would be much more manageable for me than a big school. I spent two years in Mount Carroll and then a year in England as part of a year-abroad program; then I graduated in 1969, in three years.

Mathematics is very logically self-contained and straightforward. There is little ambiguity at the college level. Even the mistakes are productive; when

I made one, the teacher could explain exactly why it was wrong and I could learn from that.

With a subject like history, on the other hand, the material doesn't arrange itself. You have to figure out which events and circumstances, of all the things that happened, were relatively significant and how they all related to one another. I was getting, from reading, as much information as the other students were, but since I was not hearing the teachers' explanations, I was essentially on my own trying to make sense out of a huge mountain of historical facts.

My first priority was math, because I could do well in it without the kind of overwhelming work other subjects took, and I thought that was where most of the job possibilities were. I was also interested in pursuing English at a more advanced level, but as it turned out I didn't do that. One reason is that I didn't connect with any of my English professors in college. I basically had the same problem with English in college that I had with every other subject, except math, in high school and college; I couldn't hear enough of what the teacher said to respond in an adequate way. What saved me was my writing ability; I got Bs in English because I wrote well.

But I did connect with a math professor and became as much of a math major as Shimer's curriculum allowed. The subject became more and more intriguing and I decided to try to go to grad school in that area, although I expected that sooner or later I would become a computer person. It was 1969, the dawn of the computer age, and I had gotten summer jobs working with some early computers owned by the Illinois state government, for which both my parents worked at the time.

The University of Chicago mathematics department admitted me as a graduate student on probationary status, taking advanced undergraduate courses. After all, my undergraduate degree was a B.A. with a concentration in Natural Sciences, but they figured that anybody who could get a B.A. at the age of 19 was probably worth a shot. I sealed my welcome by getting As in the first three courses I took, so I was invited into the regular graduate program.

Then something interesting happened. By going into the regular program, I went from basically being a real "star" at Shimer — probably the best math student there at the time — to the University of Chicago, one of the best math departments in the country, where I was merely average. Here I was with people who were just as smart as I was and with people who were definitely smarter at my best subject. The competition had gotten serious.

I survived. I kept on, expecting to flunk out, but I wasn't going to give up. I made it to the end of the second year and I was invited to come back in a quite direct way: they offered financial support as the DVR grants were running out.

Surviving at the University of Chicago was due, in part, to the work ethic I had learned growing up because I was deaf and was forced to work harder. Of course, it helped that the subject became, if anything, more interesting the farther I went into it. I kept at it and got my Ph.D. in 1977; it took eight years in all.

Even then, I hadn't yet decided on an academic career. Basically, I had decided to follow this as far as I could — and I had gone farther than I had really expected. I wasn't aiming for a goal; I was just trying to keep it going as long as I could.

Mathematics at that level had become really, deeply interesting to me, but there was something else: The University of Chicago, beginning with the math department and branching out, was the most stimulating intellectual environment I'd ever been in. There were just all kinds of really interesting people I got to hang out with socially. So, all in all, it was a terrific life. That was my milieu.

❧

Eventually, it was time to finish. I had proved what I was trying to prove and was awarded my doctorate. A year or so earlier, I had really started thinking about what I wanted to do. My friends wanted to be professors and keep working on interesting mathematics. I realized that if I wanted to do that I would have to choose an academic environment. I thought I should at least try this kind of work.

By this time, all my contemporaries were teaching calculus courses, and I wasn't because I was deaf. My advisor started seriously leaning on the person who was in charge of assigning graduate students to teach undergraduate courses. But he was adamant — he would not budge. As far as I know, it was the only instance in my career of anti-deaf prejudice.

It wasn't prejudice in the normal sense of the word. There was genuine uncertainty whether I could do it. I didn't know the answer myself. I wanted to find out, my advisor thought I would probably be fine, but this guy didn't want to take the chance.

What eventually happened is that my advisor managed to get me a job at the University of Indiana branch at Gary, where I taught a low-level class. Rather to my surprise, I did a competent job. I discovered that I could do it, and equally important, I acquired a track record. By the way, I was mediocre, a rank beginner, but in later years, after I'd compared notes with my friends and had seen other beginning teachers, I realized that for a beginner, I'd done well.

Part of it was the fact that it was all new to me because, from high school on, I wasn't really sure what teachers said in class since I was never really hearing them. I had no real idea what a normal lecture was like, what a professor said to the class for an hour, how much material to cover, how to pace it. I had no idea, so I just winged it, using whatever I could think of to get the job done.

I had an odd advantage: I knew that I didn't know anything about what a teacher did. Comparing notes later with my friends, I discovered that when they began, they didn't know what teachers did either. They'd begun teaching with great confidence, only to realize with chagrin, some time into the job, that hearing lectures and giving them are quite different things. We were all beginners, but I knew it going in and it took my friends a while to learn it.

In any event, I prepared lectures that I'd read straight from my notes. I assigned homework and read it all carefully, using it as feedback. I discovered that I could handle the technical problems of getting questions in class. I could hear questions from the front two rows and that was generally enough.

I got better at teaching. At the first class, I always tell students to raise their hands if they have questions, so I know who's talking. Like math lecturers in general, I walk back and forth writing at the board rather than sitting in one place, so when students do have questions, I just walk up to them in order to establish a good speech reading distance for me. And the students quickly learn to raise their hands so I'll come to them. Every now and then, I have a student with a difficult accent. When that happens, I usually just look at a nearby student, and almost every time, that student will repeat the question.

My first job out of graduate school was a two-year assignment as a temporary assistant professor at Rutgers University in New Brunswick, New Jersey. It was a very good place to go right out of graduate school, while I was still learning.

But after the two years, I wanted to live in a big city again. I applied for a permanent position to 63 big-city universities. Howard University made me the best offer, and Washington, D.C., looked like a reasonable place to live, so I came. Howard turned out to be a good place for me, and I'm a tenured professor now. As for Washington, well, I met Becky here, our children Genevieve and Claire came along, and for quite some time now I've been feeling as much a part of my own family and our community as I did back in Chicago where they cheered for my hearing aid.

&

I'd had almost no contact with the world of deafness, and most of the few deaf people I did encounter were as mainstreamed as I was, until sometime in the early '80s, out of the blue, I was invited to join the Alexander Graham Bell Association for the Deaf and Hard of Hearing, with its headquarters in Washington, D.C. I do think community service is important, so I accepted. I went to meetings, served on a committee or two, and then went to my first National Convention in 1986, mainly because it was in Chicago and it would give me a chance to go home to see my family.

What happened was interesting. I was picked to join the Board of Directors. I also wound up talking to some other deaf adults — and a lot of parents of deaf children and teachers of deaf students. It was clear that meeting successful mainstreamed deaf people was important to them, and reassuring: I had made it, so it's actually possible. It wound up being a very emotional thing for me. In fact, it totally blindsided me. I was accustomed to high-powered math conferences, but this was the most draining conference I ever attended.

I'm not really that interested in deafness — it doesn't define me — but I've discovered that I am very interested in encouraging other parents who want to give their deaf children that great thing my parents gave me as a deaf person: spoken language, and thereby direct access to the wide world.

Michael Janger

WASHINGTON, D.C.

Michael Janger is Manager of Finance of the Government Division at West Group, an information solutions provider for legal and business professionals. He supervises financial strategy, analysis, planning and budgeting for government markets across the U.S. A native of Westchester County, New York, he received his B.A. from Brown University in 1990, and an M.B.A. from the Wharton School of the University of Pennsylvania in 1997. He lives in Washington, D.C.

ക

I turned 30 about two months ago. A milestone like that really makes you think about what you want to do with your future. I'm using the occasion to think hard about the rest of my life: I picture myself in a retirement home in the year 2053, regretting the fact that there are some things I should have done earlier. The way I look at it, the time to get started is *now*.

I was born deaf with a hearing loss of 100 decibels. My mother had German measles when she was pregnant with me; it was during the rubella epidemic of the '60s. I was diagnosed with a profound hearing loss at nine months and fitted with hearing aids when I was about one-and-a-half years old.

During my childhood, my family lived in Hastings-on-Hudson in Westchester County, north of New York City. When I was one year old, my parents enrolled me in an oral program at the Lexington School for the Deaf in New York City, where I was a student until I was four. I remember thinking to myself at that time that "People do not wear hearing aids out-

Michael Janger

side Lexington School. But in Lexington, people do." In other words, if a hearing person walked into Lexington School, he or she automatically wouldn't be able to hear anything, because he wasn't wearing hearing aids. In other words, my mother wouldn't be able to hear me when she came to pick me up at school.

But in reality, hearing people didn't need hearing aids because they could hear. I don't remember it ever hitting me that I couldn't hear as well as other people; instead, the realization was more gradual. I do remember asking my parents questions like, "Do they have a hearing aid that can help me hear while watching TV, or talking on the telephone?" It was in the days before closed captioning and telephone relay.

Basically, I was a kid who wore hearing aids in a hearing environment. Everyone else in my family is hearing, including my two brothers, Ted, who is seven years older, and Matthew, who is five years older. Starting in kindergarten, my parents enrolled me in a mainstreaming program with other deaf kids in the neighboring school district of Edgemont. I was at Edgemont until seventh grade, when I transferred to the junior high school in my hometown of Hastings.

I socialized with hearing kids more than 90 percent of the time at Edgemont. The only difference was, we had a teacher for the deaf who worked with and tutored us. Looking back, these were the best years of my childhood; I had a great, close-knit group of hearing friends *and* a group of really good deaf friends. It was a strong, supportive combination of both.

Also at Edgemont, between second and sixth grade, I got involved in competitive soccer, basketball, and baseball teams. I developed really strong friendships with my teammates, especially in soccer. My soccer teams — named "The Force" after the movie, *Star Wars* — made it to the championship for three straight years. The Force dominated everyone on the field, with the notable exception of a devastating 0-7 loss to the Hurricanes when an easy ball rolled gently through the goalie's legs. In fifth grade, we even made it to the Westchester County finals.

The winning spirit of The Force, in many ways, was a product of our ability to support each other on and off the field, regardless of the fact that one of us was hearing-impaired. We were a strong, tightly-knit group that spent a lot of time together. Often times today, when I think about teamwork and the ability to work together though difficult times, I think of my days with The Force.

Those were really wonderful times I had at Edgemont. In many ways, it is because I had an active social life there, not only in sports but in the entire community.

Starting in seventh grade, when I transferred to Hastings, things changed. My new classmates had never grown up with deaf or hard-of-hearing people, and they were now entering their teenage years. Academics were not an issue for me as far as my hearing impairment was concerned. I did well in the classroom, but I was always sure to face the blackboard, to always watch the teacher and not sit too far back in class. Socially, however, Hastings was a completely different word from Edgemont, and my move into a very unfamiliar world was amplified by the start of my teenage years — certainly a very difficult combination.

I recall a time in tenth grade when teachers were given a pamphlet from a deaf association. On that pamphlet, there was a long list of what teachers should do and expect with a deaf student. One of the suggestions on that list was to wear lipstick to make lip-reading easier. One teacher took this a little bit too far by daubing herself with big, bright orange-colored lipstick every day — maybe a little too much lipstick. When I saw this pamphlet a few months later, I was embarrassed by the fact that it was distributed; I wanted the teachers to focus more on my academic potential than on my deafness.

The best teachers were the ones who were always sure to face the class when talking, so I could see them — and yet at the same time, made sure not to show favoritism toward me. I just wanted to fit in and didn't want special treatment. The best teachers I had were aware of that. Often times, those teachers who focused on the relative strengths and weaknesses of the individual students in their classes usually were the most effective. They made the material interesting and stimulating for everyone.

One teacher in particular — a history teacher — made a real difference. His course was literally the most difficult course I took in high school, and

I had to claw and scratch my way through. He was often hard to understand, because he taught the course like it was a college course with a heavily revisionist approach to history. He lectured from notes and observations, and challenged students to interpret and critique historical facts. I had a really tough time understanding him, since it was the first time I had a history teacher who didn't do the "textbook method" of teaching.

I compensated for the lack of verbal comprehension by reading literally everything in his voluminous reading list. It was an unbelievably difficult course, which is part of the reason that throughout the year I suffered from an involuntary muscle twitch above my right eye. Yet, when I look back, I think of him as one of my two favorite high school teachers: His course gave me a taste of what college courses would be like, and I was glad for the opportunity to get a dose of reality before college ever started. More importantly, he stimulated my interest in history — one that continues to this day. Whenever I have a chance, I read history books and go to museums with historical exhibits.

Just like at Edgemont, I played soccer in Hastings. But, this time, my soccer skills never developed to the competitive high-school level. I was never a first-stringer; in fact, I saw little playing time. Of course, getting involved in sports was important for achieving self-esteem and at least some social recognition, but the fact of the matter is that if you are a third-string player in a high-school environment, as I was, you don't make much headway socially.

In high school, there was a lot of social pressure, which depended on knowing where the "coolest parties" were being held, having inside information on who was going out with whom, and knowing who the BMOCs and the nerds were on the social status scale. Word-of-mouth was a very big deal in high school since there was no telephone relay or mass-market Internet at the time on which I could rely.

I didn't always know where those parties were and was never in the loop on teenage social gossip, because I found it extremely difficult to understand the feverish, energetic teenage dialogue bouncing off the walls of Hastings High School. In fact, I never knew there was such a thing as a "party" (in the high school sense without adult supervision, if you can get my drift) until eleventh grade, when a friend brought me to my first meadow party.

∽

I entered Brown University in 1986 as a freshman. Right from the beginning, the college experience was definitely very different from what I went through in high school. I was much more socially involved. While I wasn't completely "hearing" in the social context, so to speak, it was a wonderful, liberating experience for me to meet people and socialize as I never could in high school. I was able to respond much better to the social life at Brown. As in high school, the academics, though more challenging, weren't an issue.

At Brown, people were more accepting of me and of my deafness; although this was of course a predominantly white Ivy League university, my friends came from a wide variety of backgrounds and were "street smart." They were a much more diverse group than in high school and wouldn't hesitate to express their views, which is very typical of the Brown University environment. And they accepted you for who you were. This was an attitude that helped me thrive socially.

I got involved in several activities at Brown. I was a photographer with the college newspaper, *The Brown Daily Herald*, and was part of the Orientation and Welcoming Committee, a group of upperclassmen who organized orientation activities for incoming freshmen.

But the activity that I was by far the most involved in was the task of helping develop a support service system for deaf students at Brown. It was a collective endeavor, which I did on my own during my first year at Brown, and eventually with other deaf students who entered Brown during my upper-class years.

At Brown, I became quite involved with computers and the Internet, which had a fraction of the interest that it has now — the pre–Yahoo days. I'd actually gotten interested in computers during high school — the old "Radio Shack Days" of computer technology when having a TRS-80 was computer nirvana. I took a computer science class as an eighth grader. I got hooked then, but then lost interest during high school when I had other more pressing issues to deal with, like getting involved socially in high school — which turned out to be a losing cause anyway.

I was a political science major at Brown. But while I was there, I took another computer science course and loved it. Around that same time, a friend introduced me to the Internet and I became involved in several subscriber groups. But it was only a passing fancy for me — in 1991, very few people bothered to get actively involved in the Internet. I quickly lost interest again, and it was not until 1995, during my first year at Wharton, that the Internet really took off as a mass medium. That's when I became genuinely interested in the Web.

So, is computer technology a particularly good career for a deaf person? The Internet has become a very accessible medium for the deaf community. At the same time, computer and Internet companies are now incorporating voice and other features that make it less accessible to deaf people. I fear that, in 10 years or so, the Internet will become less accessible to deaf people. History supports this possibility: The telegraph in the 1850s would have been a great way for deaf people to communicate, but then the telephone and radio came along and uprooted the telegraph.

Today, Web sites are incorporating more and more audio clips onto their pages. So, like in the past, there will *always* be a need for new technologies to circumvent this perpetual trend. So, as long as this trend exists, being at the leading edge of technology is always a great career for a deaf person.

After all, you want to be in the forefront of technology. It gets back to what I was saying before; one of the things I've been thinking about off-and-on is starting a high-tech company, one that could benefit people with disabilities. For a profoundly deaf person, there could be a very powerful hearing aid with a sophisticated computer chip that improves his ability to interpret sounds. For a mobility-impaired person in a wheelchair, there could be demand in the future for cheaper versions of current models that can go over inaccessible curbs and enable hiking in mountains over rough terrain.

College was great, but challenging for several reasons. First, classes are generally bigger. Also, they are more lecture- and seminar-oriented, making the information more interpretive, which is the major difference from high school classes. I used oral interpreters and notetakers during my first two years, and sign language interpreters during my last two years.

Oral interpreters are certified through a program affiliated with the Rochester Institute of Technology called the Registry of Interpreters for the Deaf. But the oral interpreters I had during my first two years of college were *not* certified — none were available in Rhode Island at the time, and I had to make do with sign language interpreters who mouthed the words. They certainly helped in transmitting the information to me, but it was a major energy drain to have unqualified oral interpreters day-in and day-out. It forced me to keep watching pairs of lips for three to four hours a day, which gets very, very tiring.

Given the oral interpreting situation, and because I really needed to get the best value out of my education during the limited time I had in college, I opted to learn sign language in order to get the most out of the sign language interpreters. Real-time captioning was still not commercially available back in the late-1980s and early-1990s, so sign language interpreters were my best option. By 1995, real-time captioning had become more popular and more commercially available. I took real-time captioning at Wharton in 1995, and this was a real godsend for me. Real-time captioning saved me a lot of energy and a lot of time otherwise spent studying.

Learning sign wasn't difficult. Growing up deaf, you are more visually-oriented. Looking back, I think that learning sign language was more than just a way to utilize sign language interpreters in my college classes. It became a tool for understanding different cultures within the deaf community.

Yes, I believe very strongly in the oral method of communication, but I also believe in the power of understanding different cultures. How can you form an opinion about signers in the deaf community if you don't know sign language? In the deaf community, I feel it's imperative to know different cultures, especially when it comes to being politically active and pushing for common initiatives like defending the rights of people with disabilities under the Americans with Disabilities Act and promoting consistent and high-quality closed captioning on television shows. It also helps us find common ground on issues that are controversial within the deaf community.

The Alexander Graham Bell Association for the Deaf and Hard of Hearing hosts an international convention every two years. Traditionally, the National Association for the Deaf (NAD) hosts its own international convention at roughly the same as the Bell Association meeting. I've been told by many oral friends that I should not go to the NAD convention.

In fact, despite my strong advocacy of oral education, I think I would be missing out by avoiding the NAD convention. If you want to understand your partners in the deaf community, you need to be there. We will always be debating various issues and working together to expand common issues in disabilities and disability-related interests. We're going to be in it with them forever, so it's to everyone's advantage to get to know one another.

Signers are very proud of their culture and their identity. It's difficult for many of them to see the benefits of oral communication, and yet it's difficult for me to understand the signers' own benefits of being in their culture. I try to take a very practical view of what's going to happen, but at the same time, I believe very strongly in the oral method and try to get people to understand my perspective.

Signers will think the same way about the sign language approach to education, and they're equally justified in doing so and feel as strongly about it as I do. The oral method has not worked for everyone, and so it is not a cure-all for everyone. I see oralism as a viable and successful option among many different viable and successful options for educating the deaf. I try to share with first-time parents of deaf children the experience of what worked best for me, and enable them to make the best and the most informed decision about which educational approach to pursue for their deaf children. At the same time, I support research that will hopefully improve oral and auditory/verbal educational methods for future generations.

❧

I was on the Executive Committee of A.G. Bell's Deaf and Hard of Hearing Section (DHHS) for four years. It's a group of oral deaf people with whom I share common interests, and gives us a forum to share our common experiences with the hearing world, especially first-time parents of deaf children, and to promote the oral education method.

I went to my first A.G. Bell Convention in 1984, when I was 15. It was in Portland, Oregon, all the way across the country from my hometown in New York, and I didn't want to go. Because of my misplaced pride, no doubt aided by teenage angst, I wanted to stick with my hearing friends. But my parents gave me no choice, saying that they had already bought the airplane tickets. They dragged me kicking and screaming to Oregon. In hindsight, I'm glad they did.

It was an eye-opening experience. Remember, I was in high school at that time, which was a very difficult time for me. I went to very few parties and didn't have any close friends. Yet, here in Portland were a whole bunch of people like me. When we were together, it was just a great feeling to do things together without feeling any crippling social pressure. It just felt normal. That convention helped restore my faith in myself, and I became confident for the first time since my childhood days at Edgemont.

That experience was really my first full-scale exposure to an oral hearing-impaired culture. It's a culture that allows me to have other deaf friends with whom I can share common experiences, while continuing to interact as much as I can with the hearing world. Being in this culture gives me a perspective that is different from the perspective of deaf people who prefer signing. I have gone to every convention since Portland. Every time I go, it is a personal renewal.

One of my strong desires is to be able to help others who might be where I was in high school. Let's face it, as a deaf teenager, you're going to be teased. What it takes is the self-confidence to go through the teasing and prodding. I want to be there as a resource to teenagers, to make it a little easier for them and to be a role model. That way, they get to meet oral deaf adults and share their stories.

At recent Bell Association conventions, there was a program for oral hearing-impaired teenagers called "Leadership Opportunities for Teens" or LOFT. It is focused on leadership training for teens. I find it a fantastic way for oral deaf teenagers to meet their peers, while developing the tools and the skills they need to be successful in the hearing world.

At the 1986 Bell Convention in Utah, one teenager from the LOFT program came up to me and asked about learning French. He didn't have the confidence he needed to learn French; he doubted that deaf people could do it. When I asked him why he wanted to learn French, he said "because I want to."

I told him that was as good a reason as any to do it. He seemed to feel better about his decision afterwards. I wonder if it helped give him a push to do what he really wanted to do. After all, I feel if there's something you really want to do, you should just go ahead and do it.

Take a deaf friend of mine: He always loved doing stocks; it was something he enjoyed doing since he was 11 years old. He had confidence, he was persistent and he was going after something that he loved doing, and was good at it. He became a successful investment banker in Hong Kong, and today runs his own hedge fund in California.

In the highly verbal, highly competitive, and highly communicative world of investment banking, he took a chance and it worked. This reminds me: I wonder what ever happened to the guy who wanted to learn French?

Karen Kirby

San Antonio, Texas

Karen Kirby is a former chairperson of the Alexander Graham Bell Association's Oral Hearing Impaired Section. A native of Ocala, Florida, she has been a Bell Association member for more than 20 years and has participated in panels, presentations and leadership training.

Kirby received her master's degree in guidance and counseling from the University of North Florida, and today is a high school counselor in San Antonio, Texas She and her husband, Tony, recently became parents of a baby boy, Cassady, born in October 1999.

I was about three years old when I got my hearing aid. For me, it was like the day I was born because I really don't have much recollection of anything before then. I didn't realize I wasn't hearing anything before I was aided.

I'm not really sure if I was deaf at birth. There is a possibility that I could have had a viral infection when I was a baby and lost my hearing that way. At the time, I had what I believe was a mild-to-moderate loss; although today, I have a loss in the 96-decibel range, which makes it severe/profound.

I lived in Ocala, Florida, with my mother and father and my brother, who is two years younger than me. It's a long time ago — more than 40 years — but I remember a couple of things in particular after I was diagnosed: First, my parents and I visited the St. Augustine (Florida) School for the Deaf and Blind and I can remember not liking it very much. I don't really remember why I didn't like it — I just didn't feel comfortable there. But it didn't make much difference; the authorities told my parents they wouldn't accept me for the school anyway. They reasoned I could learn to speak because I had enough hearing.

The only significant thing I remember happening around the time is my mother's grandmother — my great-grandmother — telling us about a woman in Jacksonville named Mrs. Carter who could work with me. Mrs. Carter was a teacher of the deaf, and we decided to go ahead and contact her. She gave me speech and language training up until I was ready for kindergarten.

When I was about four, my family moved me to Jacksonville — about two hours northeast of Ocala. I went to live with my great-grandmother and grandmother, who lived together, and to take classes with Mrs. Carter. At first, my parents couldn't afford to go with me; then, a year or so later, my mom, dad and brother moved to Jacksonville. They wanted to be with me.

In Jacksonville, my parents enrolled me in a private school for kindergarten through second grade; and then, starting in third grade, in a public school. The important thing was that it was all mainstreamed. I had to sit in the front row to see the teacher better, but I was never treated like I was different. Although they were very strict, the teachers were skilled and good for me as well.

My family life had some ups and downs. My mom and dad divorced when I was about seven, and dad moved back to Ocala, where he ran a billboard business. But I still had a family network. My stepfather, who was a very laid-back, quiet man, was the one who would take the time to visit the school and meet with the teachers.

I also had a great-grandmother, who became my mentor and role model. That, along with my stepfather, who always encouraged me to speak up for myself, which really helped. Looking back, it *was* a support network, which is so very important to achieving confidence.

At the time, that was particularly important because, back then, I was a bit of a tomboy who found that the hearing aids tended to get in the way of athletics. Sometimes, I just lost them. That's when my great-grandmother pulled me aside one day — I must have been about nine at the time — and said she was going to ask me some questions.

First, she asked me, "Why do people wear glasses?" "So, they can see better," I said. Then, she asked me, "Why do people wear leg braces?" "So, they can walk better," I told her.

Then, it just hit me: The same principle applies for hearing aids. "People wear them to hear better," I told myself. I didn't have a problem with wearing hearing aids after that, or since. It was no longer a question: I'd wear them.

My hearing accommodations were minimal at the time. I had body aids — hearing aids in both ears, connected to a chest FM transmitter by a cord. It so happened that a lot of the kids in the neighborhood were boys. They were rough and tumble and could be bullies. I had to learn to defend myself.

It wasn't until I was much older that I developed an appreciation for the way I grew up. I'm referring to family discipline: That was a big part of the way I was raised. Now you can't do that — not with all these child abuse complaints — however, it was the way I grew up. I was given a lot of chores and I think every child should benefit from that. Discipline was a big key.

Parents should keep that in mind. One of the biggest problems today in raising a hearing-impaired child is that parents want to do everything for their child. I suppose this is mostly the way today's children are raised, given every toy and benefit their parents use to win their attention. Parents who overcompensate for their handicapped children become part of the problem. To a certain extent, such children should learn to get along by themselves.

I was in the seventh grade when we moved to Chester, a town in central Georgia, where my stepfather, a banker, had a business opportunity. That was the start of a couple of different moves for us and different schools for me during the next couple of years. Yet, I was still mainstreamed and managed to do fairly well.

We moved again the following year, this time south to a town on the Georgia-Florida state line called Folkston, where my stepfather was transferred, again. And it's there that I had my first really negative school experience.

Up to then, I'd always done well in school. But in Folkston, my teachers and classmates didn't know what to make of me; I think they were even a little scared of me, having never known a deaf person before. Like the other schools, I got to sit in the front row in class. And I had a guidance counselor who helped me after classes in whatever areas I needed.

But they really weren't prepared for me. You have to remember that my speech still wasn't clear, and some thought I was retarded. That may have been the difference between being in a big city as opposed to a small town. People in Folkston with a population of 2,200 just weren't used to somebody like me.

✧

My guidance counselor in Folkston was significant in one important respect. He was a Beatles lover — this was about the time that they hit it big — and he was the one who actually exposed me to the music and got me reading the words. In his office, he kept one of those early tape players that would record on a large spool. He'd have me put on the headphones and just listen to the music. Sometimes, I'd read the lyrics on the sheet. It's how I really got interested in listening to music, as opposed to just dancing to it.

It was all so important because music was a big part of my home life while I was growing up. My mother always had a radio on and I just liked to listen to music with her. As I never understood the words, listening like that really deepened my appreciation of music. More on that later.

Otherwise, the situation wasn't good. We had to do something. We had to make a decision. So, my mother got special permission to take me back to the Jacksonville school in ninth grade. Jacksonville is a big city and there were more services there. I spent a year there and then went back to Georgia, where I spent the final three years of high school and graduated. In retrospect, I wish I hadn't, but that's what happened.

I wasn't a particularly strong student in high school. But I was fairly active socially, particularly as a cheerleader. I didn't have a lot of friends at school although I went to all the parties. I had one really good friend through high school and we did everything together. Her parents had an ice skating rink, so I would go skating unless I had a game to travel to for cheerleading.

My parents helped me tremendously. There's that network again: When I went to out-of-town games, they would drive me there; they had to take me until I could drive myself because none of the other girls ever invited me to ride with them. It didn't bother me, since my brother was in the band and he always rode with us, too. It was easier for me to have Mom or Dad take me to away games.

I graduated. I learned later — and only after talking to my mother — that throughout high school, the guidance counselor told her that due to my disability, he thought I'd never advance beyond homemaker. The other thing I later learned was his belief that I'd never make it to college. He was already trying to set my limits — all this from somebody who thought I was retarded. So, by graduating — and then by enrolling at the University of Georgia that summer — I quickly achieved what at least one person said I could never do.

My scores weren't high enough to get into the regular program at Georgia. However, my stepfather believed I could do it. He also believed I needed a summer job to earn some money of my own. I remember working that summer when I was 15. Paying my way was part of the work ethic my family taught me. I took that to heart.

Even so, I was unprepared for the University. I was allowed to take two courses and frankly, I was a little overwhelmed. I knew what I wanted to do, which was go into children's education, but it was a huge university and classes were in big lecture halls, which made it particularly difficult for me. I was happy there, but I was also frustrated and recognized that I probably needed to attend a smaller college. Then, through a student of Mrs. Carter's — a girl I had known years before in Jacksonville — I found out about that kind of university, East Tennessee State University in Johnson City, Tennessee.

Not much time had elapsed. It was still the summer after I graduated from high school and I started right away in the fall at East Tennessee State. Tutoring was offered but I didn't need it, because I found the school was just what I needed. I passed the first semester with an "A" average. I went out for sports and played on the tennis team.

I loved it. It was a much smaller university than the University of Georgia. My adviser was wonderful and made sure I had the right kind of classes and taught me to go to the new professors at all my classes and ask if a notetaker could be designated. The teachers were very good about that and supportive in general.

The notetakers helped. So do things like oral interpreters for deaf students. Thinking back, I did well academically — except for high school, when I just missed out on so much. If I could go back in time, I'd use an interpreter in high school, the way I did in college. Today, there are interpreters, along with real-time captioning and note takers; there are just so many options that can help hearing-impaired students.

To succeed, I still had to believe in myself. After my first year of college, my adviser suggested I change my major from education to physical education. He thought I'd be a better teacher in phys-ed because I was so athletic. I appreciated his view as I'm an athletic person, but I thought that reading and writing were so much more important than physical activity. I decided to stick to the program where I had started.

Ultimately, I chose education because I wanted to be in the classroom. I knew from the time I was about 12 or 13 that I wanted to be a teacher; I'd never felt any limitations and I never felt that my teachers treated me any differently than anyone else. I knew that teaching was what I wanted to do.

Of course, I knew that I couldn't hear as well as others. But I didn't grow up with the label "deaf" or "hard of hearing." Still, my adviser urged me to reconsider and said I should think it over during summer break. And then he suggested if I still really wanted to be a teacher, I should consider being a teacher for the deaf.

He thought that I, as a deaf person, wouldn't be able to teach in the public schools. To me, that was a reality shock because in a way, yes, I was deaf—legally and audiologically—but I never grew up thinking of myself as deaf, nor did I grow up with any sense of limitation. His insistence prompted a kind of identity crisis for me when I got home for the summer, which, coincidentally was about the time I was due to attend my first A.G. Bell Convention.

It was 1974 and I was going with Mrs. Carter to the convention, which was in Atlanta that year. This traced to the year before when I was a high school senior and had attended the American Speech and Language Association state convention in St. Petersburg, Florida. There, I had been part of a panel of deaf teenagers and children. Because I had done well, I was asked to participate in the same kind of panel for A.G. Bell in Atlanta.

On the way to the convention, I remember telling Mrs. Carter about the dilemma of doing so well in school, yet having my adviser pushing me to change my major. Mrs. Carter was on my side and told me I could do whatever I wanted to do. So, I asked her was I really deaf? She told me I was, but "audiologically" deaf. Then, she told me that in my case we just didn't need to use that kind of label most of the time. I did so well that people couldn't even tell I was hard of hearing or deaf. In her mind, I was simply a person with a hearing loss.

That sunk in and so I kind of left the issue alone after that. We got to the convention hotel in Atlanta, and there I was, suddenly meeting all these different types of people — parents of deaf children, deaf professionals, you name it. I was overwhelmed at seeing all these deaf adults because I'd never had that kind of exposure to deaf people before. I'd had some contact as had other students of Mrs. Carter's, but it had never occurred to her to have successful deaf adults come to meet some of the younger kids. That's done a lot today, and it would have been helpful in my case to show that I could be whatever I wanted to be.

I was completely overwhelmed by the convention. I was awed to find out that any of these people could be anything they wanted to be: a lawyer, a doctor, an architect or a nurse. It was all so encouraging and confidence-building. I remember meeting a deaf woman there who taught in public school and overheard me telling somebody about my experience with my adviser who had wanted me to change my major, because he thought I wouldn't be able to handle teaching in a public school. This teacher introduced herself and told me that I had everything I needed to be a successful teacher in the classroom. I never forgot that.

Prior to that, I had no real exposure to deaf adults. I grew up in a hearing role and was raised to believe that I was just like everybody else. I couldn't hear everything, and I knew that. It didn't bother me that I wore a hearing aid.

The convention inspired me. I went back to school and told my adviser that I was going to be a teacher in a public school. He still refused to think I could do it — but he couldn't stop me from trying. Three years later, I graduated with a B.A. degree in elementary education. In addition, I played on the tennis team for three years and improved each year.

During my senior year, I knew that I was going to have to do an internship, which required classroom teaching. For that, I was sent to an open fourth-grade classroom, which required some adjustments and some quick thinking: First, I had to block out all the extra noise that comes in the classroom. Second, I was never told that my group of kids was gifted. I remember them asking me questions like "Why do you talk so funny?" and "Where are you from?" I just laughed and told them I was from Florida. They just thought I talked the way I do because of where I'm from.

Meantime, I wore my hearing aid and just focused on teaching in a regular classroom. These gifted kids were really something: I saw how quickly they would write everything down and how fast they'd write on the board. Their questions were very good. At end of the year, I told them my surprise — that I was deaf. They told me there was no way I could be deaf because I heard everything they said. "Not necessarily," I told them. "I lipread."

So I graduated in 1977 and moved back to Ocala to teach fifth grade. I also got married; I've been married and divorced twice. It was also around the time I was teaching back in Florida that I attended the 1980 A.G. Bell Convention in Houston and met a college professor from the University of North Florida in Jacksonville. He got me thinking about going back to college to get a master's in deaf education.

That coincided with some growing problems with my own hearing. I needed a new hearing aid at the time and wondered how long I could teach in a classroom. I thought maybe I should go back to college at night, while continuing to teach during the day. By that time I was divorced. I started out on my master's for deaf education, but only lasted one semester. I was encouraged to change goals once again because of the success I had in counseling parents.

What happened was that the school principal made some comments about some parent conferences I'd had, saying that one of my strengths was that I was really consistent with how I worked with the parents. It got me to thinking and spearheaded a change in the focus of my graduate work to counseling. I'd just as soon be a teacher and use some of my counseling skills; and so I did, while continuing to teach. Then after three years, I moved to Jacksonville to attend school full time. Two years later, I got my degree.

After getting my degree, I accepted an offer to work at Sunshine Cottage School for the Deaf in San Antonio. I had discovered through the Dallas chapter of the A.G. Bell Association that the school was looking for a hearing-impaired person to be its counselor. I spent seven years in the deaf program at Sunshine Cottage, doing far more than being a counselor. Instead, I was everything: a resource teacher one year, mainstream teacher another year, itinerant teacher yet another. I did whatever was needed.

But I wanted a full-time counseling job, and I wanted to go back in public schools, particularly because under the Americans with Disabilities Act, so many things have changed. So, starting in 1996, I went to Foxlands Elementary, in San Antonio, where today I'm a counselor to the school's 925 students.

It's a challenge. Foxlands has a program for parents of (special) children up to age three in which parents are taught how to work with their children at home. For the children, there's a pre-school program for three to five year olds along with additional programs when they enter school.

The philosophy is to give the kids enough training so that they can be mainstreamed. For deaf children in particular, we need to make it possible, because they will benefit more in the hearing world than in a deaf environment. I really believe that every child should have that foundation and should be mainstreamed as early as possible.

Deaf children will pick up a lot more of the language among their hearing friends. It's a struggle and I'm not suggesting it's easy. It wasn't easy for me either. I had to accept being made fun of and how to overcome that. But, in a lot of ways, hearing kids can go through similar things.

There are so many kids in special education, including about one-third of my school's student population. That includes programs for the physically-impaired and autistic programs. And it includes alternative learning environments for others.

My reasons for choosing this route is central to wanting to be a teacher in the first place. I can remember for the most part, a lot of my teachers didn't treat me any differently other than anyone else. I remember in elementary school that I had to read in front of the classroom, and even though I didn't pronounce all the words correctly, the teacher was there to help me.

I can remember there were times when I'd make an excuse that something was wrong with my hearing aid when I was asked to read out-loud. I hated it. I would use a dead battery in my hearing aid as an excuse to get out of reading in class. I didn't think I could speak well enough, but I did speak well. Looking back, it all makes me think how influential a good teacher can be.

⤚

There were other things that helped me along the way. I love to dance — an interest that started when I was four because my mother wanted me to have some social skills — and I continue today to enjoy dancing.

My mother was a singer and a piano player, but she didn't think I could do either one because I couldn't hear the notes. But thinking it would help me socially, she got me to learn how to dance. So, from the ages of five to 12 I took studio dance three days a week. Mom was right; it did help me and I enjoyed it.

My particular interest today is country-western dancing. I got into country about 15 years ago, when people were going through slow-dancing and disco dancing crazes. What appealed to me about country-western dancing was that there seemed to be more guys who knew how to dance that style than anything else.

Besides, I was good at it. I hooked up with a friend who taught me a lot of the techniques. Before long, I got into a contest at a club where there was a dance floor and the dance was country. I even met my second husband through country; he was a deejay at a club where we danced country.

The contest was interesting. Dancing with my friend John, we won the local contest and therefore qualified for the state competition. At this point, we figured we had to find somebody to help us choreograph certain things. In part because I couldn't hear the music and relied instead on the vibrations of the music, we hired a professional teacher to work with John on feeling the vibration of the music. Because I don't hear the tempo, it is important to be on the beat and that both partners be in sync.

The teacher told me I had the creative movement to be a good dancer. But, since John liked to do all this improvisational dancing stuff, I could never follow him because he was off beat. Finally, after working with the teacher, John finally understood where I was coming from and how important it was that we choreograph the movement we intended to do for the competition.

The teacher's advice for me was just to do whatever John asked me to do. The logic was if I started a beat, I'd be able to control it and that I would be able to get him back on the beat because he'd be able to quickly pick it up.

We practiced everywhere we could find. At the contest, there were eight finalists and we had the luck to draw the last number. Guess what? We won and part of the reason was simply that I had to do a better job than anybody else, learn the piece and the music, while adding my own creativity. I have to be able to feel the music, to feel like I'm within the beat. I'm more of a rhythm person; if I feel the beat, I'm in control. I feel really alive when I dance.

❧

Dance has been a big part of my life. I also have my two hearing dogs, who have helped me live on my own. It all started when I moved to Jacksonville back in 1980 to begin work for my master's degree. It was after my divorce and my parents told me that they were concerned about my safety. I was living alone in a big city.

I was determined to be on my own. But my dad was really concerned that as a deaf person, I wouldn't be able to hear a knock at the door or a ringing telephone. Then, I learned about the hearing dog program and that's when I applied and got Brownie, a trained German shepherd.

It makes a difference. Brownie would only bark when somebody actually knocked on the door. She'd bark to get my attention and I'd follow her. For the telephone and the smoke alarm, she'd go to the source of the sound. And again, she'd get my attention and I had to follow her to the sound.

Dogs like Brownie are trained to know what we could and couldn't hear. Owners are trained to recognize what the dog was hearing. Brownie was one year old when she came to me. She stayed with me for three years until she developed a flea allergy that grew so serious that she had to go back to Colorado, where she was trained.

So four months after I had to give up Brownie, I got Cinder and had her for 13 years, until she was put to sleep in July 1996. She had developed arthritis and was in such pain; and, of course, I'd grown so attached to her. It was a sad time for me.

I recommend these dogs for deaf people. Right now I don't have one, since in the last few years, I've been traveling a lot more. Even so, Cinder and Brownie went everywhere with me, actually, getting on the plane and sitting on the floor next to me. Usually, it would be the front seat because there's more floor space; then, they'd lay down right there.

We always flew American Airlines, which was very accommodating and whose flight attendants were always spoiling the dogs with treats. Brownie and Cinder always got to sit in the middle of the aisle when they weren't working and they were always very quiet, never once growling or barking. They're great dogs.

Different companies train hearing dogs. A lot of hearing impaired college kids have hearing dogs for protection and to help them get along. A lot of deaf people don't realize what their entitlements are. These dogs aren't pets; they're working dogs trained to help you.

At the same time, I have to admit that one of the reasons I didn't want to get another hearing dog is because I grew so attached to them. I have another dog, a pet, but I still haven't gotten a new working dog.

Karen Kirby with Cinder

❧

Like a lot of oral deaf people, I didn't learn to sign until I was an adult. It wasn't until after the A.G. Bell Convention in 1980 when I learned. I remember it well: I had gone out with a bunch of people and had some problems hearing some of these people or even lipreading because the restaurant was so dark.

When the restaurant manager came by and started signing with one of the people at the table, I was able to see it from the perspective of how my companions felt as deaf people. It helps them communicate. You have to remember I had enough hearing — and still have enough hearing — that I can generally get by without signing.

These people were oral, but they also signed. I didn't know at the time that they knew sign or that they were majoring in deaf education. And I kept asking, "What are you saying?" and "What are you all signing?" I got lost.

So, I decided to learn. I wanted to know what they were saying. Over the years, I found that it's just another language. I figured if I wanted to be an effective counselor, I needed to be able to communicate with people who sign.

But even today — on the job — I'm still not exposed to a lot of deaf people. For the most part, the deaf people I see at work come to my office because they know I can communicate with them. They generally sign and mouth the words. I sign in English, whereas they sign in American Sign-

Language or ASL. But they'll move their mouths, since I can understand lip-reading and some sign. I ask them to move their mouths and to sign at the same time to help me improve my respective skills. So we sign and communicate.

That speaks to a larger point: You need to learn to read and write in spoken language. ASL is not using English. When you pick up a book, it's in English. You can't write a letter in ASL.

I believe if you're deaf, it's a real advantage to learn signing after you learn to speak. Looking back, I wish I'd had the advantage of using interpreters. Deaf students today are fortunate to have this as an option.

People have choices. Over the years, I've met some deaf people who see that I can speak and so they say to me, "Oh, you're hearing." But I'm not. I'm deaf. There's no exact definition of the word "deaf," or the term "hard of hearing."

So why get involved in community activities? At college, people said I couldn't succeed. Today, deaf people are insisting they can. The people who said I could is the reason I'm involved in the A.G. Bell Association. Being able to talk with parents and to share my experiences as a professional and as a deaf person in the work force means I can help.

At school, I have my own phone, using the voice relay, so that I have the contact with others. I have a computer. I have a pager that works through the relay. Since I can't be reached via the intercom, callers use the relay to get me on the pager. Basically, they've thought of different ways to help us adapt, and have created an environment that works.

Basically, I'm in a position to tell today's deaf youth how we made it in school and what advantages and options they should think about to succeed as well. After all, we made it; they can, too.

Ken Levinson

SAN FRANCISCO, CALIFORNIA

Ken Levinson is a partner in a San Francisco CPA firm. He is the former Executive Director of the Children's Hearing Institute in New York City, which provides medical research into hearing loss and rehabilitation services and educational outreach for children with cochlear implants.

From 1988 to 1990, Levinson served as President of the Alexander Graham Bell Association for the Deaf and Hard of Hearing. In October 1990, as his term neared an end, he received a cochlear implant himself.

A Seattle native, Levinson is a graduate of the University of Washington and the Columbia University Graduate School of Business. He is a San Francisco–based certified public accountant and lectures around the U.S. on issues related to hearing impairment.

⟨⟩

You could say I established a claim to fame from the start: I was born on the same day as O.J. Simpson. Our lives turned out a little differently, didn't they? A healthy baby until the age of 21 months, I acquired spinal meningitis, which left me profoundly deaf.

Right from the start, there are several significant things to emphasize: First, I had a 50-word vocabulary when I lost my hearing, giving me a tremendous advantage in vocabulary over someone who is deaf from birth. The fact that when I lost my hearing, I had heard speech and already learned to speak, even to a limited extent, was important.

The other thing is that once I lost my hearing, my parents went to work with me right away. My mother later told me that she had been particularly worried that I wouldn't be able to hear music, while my father, an engineer, knew that speech and sound were connected. This was in Seattle in the late 1940s, and my father worked at Boeing Corporation. There he had a group of colleagues who built a headset and amplifier system connected to a microphone to help me hear.

The day I left the hospital, I started talking using this headset and amplifier. In a sense, it was a high fidelity hearing aid and better than the conventional kind. In hindsight, the time between when I lost my hearing and started to use this new kind of hearing aid was so minimal that I think my

Ken Levinson

mind was still recognizing sound in a similar fashion. When you talk about early intervention, I think I'm a classic case and I'm fortunate I had a father who recognized that; it was just part of his nature to keep moving ahead.

I had gotten meningitis from a boy who lived next door. He died, but the doctor who treated me in the hospital knew that the drug he administered — astreptomyacun — would take away my hearing. It was a choice between death and deafness; I think my parents knew that I was probably going to have the hearing loss. It was a situation in which they knew what was coming, and could then figure out what to do about it. I look at it as a kind of head start in a way, another of the fortunate things that happened to me.

I don't remember a lot of specifics about growing up. It *is* a long time ago. I only know from talking in recent years with my father, particularly after my mother died, that mom took me to a speech therapist in Seattle two to three times a week when I was a kid. What I do know is that lipreading was a big part of the training, because I remember working in front of a mirror and working with feeling the throat muscles and the facial muscles, making it primarily visually oriented.

As a child, I didn't really think of myself as being different from anyone else, except that I knew I didn't have the hearing that everybody else had, and that didn't make me feel good. But again, there were some other circumstances: in my school, there was a kid with polio, so he was worse off than I was. That was a physical thing you could see.

A few words about my parents: both had an equal role in helping me with my education and development. Of course, mom stayed home and dad went to work, that is, until he decided to leave Boeing to start his own business and be able to spend more time at home. It wasn't just for me, mind you, but for my brothers, Arnie, who is two-and-a-half years younger, and Mark, who is four-and-a-half years younger. Dad was just very focused on the family, and he started his own business to control his hours and spend more hours with us — all of us.

With schoolwork, dad helped me in science and math, and mom worked with me mostly on vocabulary, composition and English. Again, a fairly even distribution, which goes for my brothers as well. My parents never treated me any differently from my brothers, both of whom have normal hearing. We three kids were equal, with no special privileges for me because I couldn't hear.

That brings up an equally important point: parents should be particularly attentive to the needs of their "other" children — the ones who are not hearing impaired. I say that because, in retrospect, my hearing loss had a considerable effect on my brother, Arnie, the middle child.

The issue came up only about 10 years ago, when we were having dinner one night in California: He brought up that he did not enjoy growing up in that household. He felt a lot of anger that I was the one getting all the apples — you know, the lion's share of the attention because of my disability.

So I asked him to explain. He said if an activity centered around him, the whole family would show up, and I tended to get the attention of one parent or the other. Arnie said he had wished that dad had asked him — just him — to go fishing, but it never happened. Not that it was terrible or anything — Arnie was an All-American basketball player and president of the Boys Club and the family was always showing up at various events in which he was involved.

Mark, my youngest brother, did not express similar feelings. But Arnie perceived me as getting special attention — you probably know, "all the apples." I don't think that was necessarily the case, but he's right in that I certainly did get more attention than he did as a kid. So the concept of everybody being equal may be the ideal, but there are times when parents of hearing impaired children should remember that their "other" children have needs as well.

On the other hand, I remember somebody asking my father about the concept of "quality time." His response: "I don't believe in that." He felt there wasn't quality time, but "time period." What he meant was there was only so much to do to develop his deaf child and that he was going to do the best that he could.

I'm the eternal optimist. It's something that probably gets me in trouble at times, because I just always expect good things to happen, and goodness knows, it doesn't always happen that way. I really don't know where it comes from, other than the fact that my self-esteem was always reinforced. So, naturally I always think that I'm going to move forward in a positive manner. Attitude is so important.

As a three year old, I went to the John Tracy Clinic summer program in Los Angeles. People there, thinking that I wouldn't be able to handle a mainstream environment, actually recommended that I go to a school for the deaf. But a therapist there told my father that she thought I'd be smart enough to be mainstreamed. That's all my dad needed to hear and that started the process.

Once in school, I was always helped along by my parents, who were always very involved and met with the teachers on a regular basis. They were really on top of it, and even pulled me out of one fifth grade class and put me in another, because they felt it just wasn't working with a particular teacher. They were just making sure the placement was right.

It happened again in junior high school, where I was carrying a B+ average. My parents pulled me out and put me in a prep school, the Lakeside School in Seattle. The classes were smaller, and I'd get individualized attention. Also, they felt that I wasn't performing up to my potential and wasn't doing as well as they thought I could.

I went through phases when being deaf was tough. Junior high was especially tough; talk to anyone, deaf or hearing, and they'll tell you that can be a hard age. Sure, I was teased, but when I think back, I think of the words of my father: "Look Ken," he would say, "there's nothing I can do about your hearing loss ... I just can't go over to the store and get you new ears." Then, he pointed out, "You're one of the best trumpet players in Seattle and there are hearing kids who can't play as well as you can."

He was right. I learned the trumpet in fourth grade and I was pretty good. Musical roots, I guess: My dad has played the violin for close to 70 years. One day when I was a kid, he brought home a trumpet and I just took to it. Pretty simple really. You'd be surprised to realize how many deaf children can play musical instruments. It's not a hard thing to do; if you're deaf, you just learn to hear music differently; it doesn't mean you can't enjoy it.

I can't say exactly why my father brought home a trumpet all those years ago. I do know he had an interest in music. And maybe, just maybe, he felt that "my son can do this and we're going to prove to the world that even though he can't hear, he can play an instrument." And I could.

But playing the trumpet was important for another reason — it helped my self-esteem. I enjoyed playing it so much that I passed up Boy Scouts to spend more time practicing and going to lessons. In retrospect, maybe subconsciously, playing the trumpet was a way to avoid getting involved with a group activity.

Socializing with other kids was hard in those years. My best friend growing up was a classmate named Sol; we spent a lot of time together. But once we got to junior high school, we started growing apart. Sol started to socialize more with the girls as well as the other guys. It just wasn't the same bond: I couldn't keep up with the changing social "order" and it was hard. I can't remember too many specific examples, but I do remember that I wasn't always the favorite kid in junior high school.

I started at Lakeside in tenth grade and it made a tremendous difference. It did a lot for my self-esteem. I had one professor who made me read an essay in front of the class about myself. It came about after I had written an earlier essay that wasn't very good, so he made me rewrite the piece as an autobiographical composition, for which he gave me an A+. When I did that, it changed the entire attitude of my classmates, who, I think, got to know a little more about me. I could tell they respected me for dealing with my hearing impairment in a positive way.

All the time, I was the only deaf student in my school. In fact, I never even met another deaf person until I was 30 years old. I have to say that the more than 20 years since then have been interesting. Starting out as somebody who thought he was better than other deaf people, I have moved on to a situation in which today, I'm a Gallaudet University board member. The point is that I have come to know many deaf people with less than oral capabilities and they are just as good as me or anyone else.

I know now that there is no correlation between speech and intelligence. But by the same token, I do have an understanding of the reality of being deaf in a hearing world. The better your oral communication skills, the better your chances are in a mainstream environment. I never had a longing to belong in the "Big D" Community, as Deaf Culture is known, but I do enjoy the company of my signing friends, while really enjoying the hearing world a lot more. I can't explain it; maybe it's the way I grew up.

Even today, there are many times when I'm in a group situation and I really can't keep up with the conversation. I suppose I could sit there and wish that everybody was in the same boat as me, but that's wishful thinking. Sure, it enters my mind sometimes, but it certainly doesn't make me want to go and become a part of the Deaf Culture. I'd rather pay the price and be integrated in the hearing world.

The ideal situation would be if I encounter a situation where I'm faced with silence because I can't keep up with the group; then I could leave that room and go next door and have this nice room of deaf people with whom I could communicate. So, do I submerge myself more in the Deaf Community and then seek comfortable situations in the hearing environment? In general, I'm just much more comfortable with my hearing friends.

At the same time, I have several deaf friends with whom I am just as comfortable.

I know sign language, picking it up back in 1978. Having a hearing loss, I knew it would be neat if I knew how to sign, so I took a course, but promptly forgot most of it. Several years later, I lost pretty much the remainder of my hearing, and so I acquired an oral interpreter to help me at work. She also did sign interpreting and took some opportunities to teach me some signs. I took another signing class at U.C.L.A. in Los Angeles. It wasn't to learn sign language as a mode of communication; it was just an interest I had.

In 1988, after I became president of the Alexander Graham Bell Association, the country's leading oral deaf advocacy group, I was asked to address the National Association for the Deaf annual convention. At first, I thought I would be going into an adversarial environment. I did not sign during my speech, but I tried to do so during social situations at the convention. In a situation where you have to sign, you'd be amazed how good you can get.

One of the other things I have learned is that success, whatever way you define it, depends greatly on parental involvement. I have met thousands of parents, spoken to numerous parent groups, and have even participated in parent attitude sessions. The one bottom line to successful deaf children is parent involvement, and not, as many folks think, the maximization of oral skills. Not all successful people will follow this pattern, but it is like any other lesson in child development. Remember, they are children first and deaf second. Parent involvement is critical to the success mechanism for any child. True, there are many who succeed despite their parents, but by and large, life is a lot easier when the parents build the appropriate foundation.

I don't think I could ever have had positive self-esteem if not for the constant involvement of my parents in everything I did — and not only involvement, but encouragement to do anything I wanted to do. And guess what? It wasn't any different for my brothers. We were encouraged to try as much as we could. Dad had an expression: "If it doesn't hurt them, let them try."

I can remember when I was five years old, our family moved in the middle of my kindergarten year, from one hill to the next in our neighborhood. We couldn't change schools. We only had one car in the family and Dad needed it to work, which meant I had to take public transportation: two buses to school, transferring from one line to the next. Mom was terrified, but Dad said: "The kid is smart enough ... Just wait and see ... He will come home after school and be just fine." Well, I'm here, aren't I? Today is very different, but the point is that parents have to let their kids learn to fly on their own. Look where it got me: I recently jumped from an airplane, and the parachute worked, as you can image. Just think what my mother would have said if I told her I was doing that. But Dad would have said: "Son, it's your life ... I can't tell you what to do." Famous words, used often. He made us all figure things out and do things for ourselves. He empowered us.

When I talk to parents and even in this chapter, you don't hear much about Mom because Dad was the logical one. When he talked, it made too much sense to argue. It still does 50 years later. But Mom was very special in her own way and was very much a part of our empowerment and self-esteem. Mom passed away in 1982, but I clearly remember something the Rabbi said at her funeral: "There is a tremendous amount of love in the Levinson family and Hank (my mom) was the catalyst of that love." How true: She had her rules and many of them were hard to follow, but she really loved us all so very much. I think *that* is another secret, although it really isn't that much of a secret: When you love your children and you show them, it provides a tremendous amount of support, especially when you have to face ignorance outside the family walls. No question Dad loves us too, and we three brothers love one another, but I truly believe Mom nurtured that environment. How lucky for us after Mom died that Dad found Heartha who has kept that love flowing as well.

Let the parents make the choice they feel is best for their children. Making choices is what it is all about. In addition, let us respect those choices without criticism. Let's remember the story: "Whose Life Is It Anyway?"

I think we are beginning to see greater acceptance among deaf people with respect to cochlear implants. There is nothing different between a child with a hearing aid and one with an implant, except for two things that could affect that child's emotional development. One is a particular parent's expectation that the implant will make their child hearing. The other is the potential ostracization of a deaf youngster because he or she has an implant.

Let's face it: Implants give many people, who could not get much information from a hearing aid, the chance to get a tremendous amount of sound. For young children, this is critical. I think we will see the day — in the not-so-distant future — when implants will provide sounds of human speech almost as good as a normal hearing person. Kids who are two or three years old today will be 12, 15 or 18 when this happens. If they do not learn to listen now, they will not learn then. I can see a whole generation of deaf people being angry with their parents for not getting them implanted at earlier ages. This does not mean we go around implanting every deaf child, but it does mean we need to be forward-thinking about the technology and what it holds in store for the future of a deaf child.

A lot of kids are not necessarily going to benefit from an implant. It doesn't help everyone. If you're born into a deaf family with deaf parents, where signing is the primary means of communication, the family may not see the point of getting an implant. That may be right for their family, and I respect that.

Historically, some members of the deaf community were angry about oralism; and, it can very well be justified. Many kids in the 1960s were forced to be oral and they were forced to speak and not sign. There wasn't any freedom to do what they wanted to do and children should be allowed to express themselves. Things are much different today. Especially at A.G. Bell, people are encouraging auditory training, but not discouraging sign language.

Because group situations were hard, I tended while growing up to develop friendships on a one-to-one basis. It was manageable that way. I could handle it. It's kind of funny to think about that today: now, I have so many friends that I have the opposite problem, and I can never find time to see them. Recently, I was back in Los Angeles and I got to thinking that there I was for only 24 hours and there were going to be at least 20 people who were going to be upset with me if I didn't call them.

It was the same when I left Los Angeles to take my position at the Children's Hearing Institute in New York. Friends hosted a "going-away party" for me and it was like a wedding: I had so many good friends there that I didn't know where to stop the invitation list. Today, I have friends all over the world.

Why? Self-esteem has a lot to do with it. And I just enjoy getting involved and becoming a leader. I love networking. And I just love playing the "Six Degrees of Separation"—the idea that between you and anyone else in the world are six people at most — all which goes to show you the remarkable connections that can take place among people. Simply put, I like asking those questions — and I think those questions start leading to more friendships, because I enjoy putting mutual friends together. I find when that happens, and before you know it, everybody ends up being friends with everybody else.

When I talk to parents of hearing-impaired youngsters, one of the things I tell them is that they aren't alone. If there's a room full of those parents, I tell them that, because of the bond they're sharing, they could become the best of friends with everyone else there.

For me, a lot of my strongest friendships stem from my participation in the A.G. Bell Association. I joined in 1978, which brought my first real exposure to deaf people. It was then that I attended my first A.G. Bell Convention, it was in St. Louis and I remember being amazed at the number of remarkable people there. It was new and I just bonded with people. We had a lot in common and it just developed from there.

We deaf people frequently make the mistake of regarding a person's deafness more highly than his or her human values. We all have to remember that we're human beings first and deaf second. All the time I was growing up, even through attending graduate school at Columbia University, I didn't think of myself as being deaf. But the fact is I am deaf and I feel a real sense of obligation to give something back and share my success with younger hearing-impaired people.

There is my involvement with A.G. Bell, of course. And when at Columbia, I called the Lexington School for the Deaf in New York City and volunteered. It was something I wanted to do. One night a month, I went there to play with a group of six or seven deaf children. And when I moved to Los Angeles, one of the first things I did was call the John Tracy Clinic to volunteer there as well. Community involvement is simply something that I enjoy. It's rewarding.

In some ways, there's no secret to success in the mainstream. As a deaf person, I had to work hard, three times as hard as anybody else. The strange thing is now I don't feel I have to work as hard as anybody else: I feel I can do better than most people even while working less than they do. I think that a work ethic helped me in high school, at Lakeside Prep School in Seattle, and at the University of Washington.

Because of the way I learned to work in high school, college was much easier. I started out studying architecture at the University of Washington, and after a year or so of not being able to draw a damn thing, I switched to accounting. That became my major and I graduated in 1969. Later, I received an M.B.A. from Columbia University, in 1971.

After Columbia, I worked for Price Waterhouse on Wall Street for a couple of years and, in 1974, transferred to their San Francisco office, where I worked until 1977. Then, I joined the Northrop Corporation in Los Angeles as a senior auditor, becoming manager of the department after a year or so. I stayed there for 10 years and left to start my own business, and eventually a C.P.A. partnership with friends. I stayed until 1996, when I moved to New York to become Director of the Children's Hearing Institute. Now, I am back in San Francisco, hoping to develop a specialty in business valuations.

Obviously, academics are important. No doubt about it. But one of the things I tell parents of hearing impaired children is that academics are not the key; the key is to develop people skills. So it's what you appear to be — and not what you really are — that counts. Of course, you have to back up that appearance with ability, but it's how you appear to people that's really important. And that is why better speech skills enhance your chances in the mainstream: to a hearing person, you appear to be a lot more self-confident than you might actually be.

After I graduated from the Columbia Business School and was interviewing for jobs, I had people from several firms tell me they weren't hiring me because I was hearing impaired. But one of the things that the interviewer at Price Waterhouse, where I was hired, told me is that I impressed them because it was clear that at the University of Washington and at Columbia, I was a campus jock and involved in all kinds of activities. They could see I was a leader — and that told them that I could deal well with people, despite being deaf.

It was the same at the University of Washington, where I was vice president of Beta Alpha Psi, the honorary accounting fraternity and had all the major accounting firms recruiting me. But I had already decided I was going to graduate school, so I never had gone through the complete interview process.

Take a look at Stanford, Harvard, Princeton or Yale and take a look at the people they recruit out of high school: They're not just straight "A" students; they're active on campus. The recruiters know it's the out-of-the-classroom stuff that will make them leaders in the working world. Think about it: Despite all the talk about the importance of academic excellence, the ultimate success of a university is really marked by what its graduates do in the working world.

Sure, the academics are important — you don't want your child to get a 2.5 grade point average — but I would rather have a kid with a 3.5 G.P.A.

who is active in many activities, as opposed to a kid with a 4.0 who hasn't joined anything.

❧

Deafness is a constant hindrance in the business world. It's something hearing-impaired people just have to accept. I can understand most, but not all people. Recently, I had a meeting with a group of people, all of whom knew each other; they were speaking so rapidly that I couldn't stop it or follow what was going on. The people there knew that I'm hearing impaired, but I think they just forgot about it as they were talking and throwing out ideas. That happens all the time.

But there are other times when being deaf actually helps. Yes, it helps. I go to conferences, and I may not need an interpreter, but I make sure I have one anyway; in fact, I always have an interpreter in a place where I want to do networking because I have found it makes me stand out. It prompts people to approach me; I'm a bit different and it gives me opportunities and advantages that wouldn't otherwise present themselves.

An example: I was at a conference a few years ago and happened to meet one of the presenters, the woman who invented "Barney," the purple dinosaur for children. It's not that I particularly wanted to meet her, but when I was introduced, she recognized me immediately because I had been sitting up front with an interpreter during her presentation. I stood out and it helped.

After all, we live in a world today in which people are much more understanding and curious about people with disabilities. They even look with admiration at people with disabilities — something I discovered when I went back to my old high school in 1993 to give the commencement address as "Alumnus of the Year." The funny thing is people told me that they really admired me even back then — although nobody told me back in school.

Finding that out was really tremendous. When I went back to Seattle, to get the award, a few of my old classmates threw a party for me. One classmate, who flew in from Florida just for the party, told me that he really looked up to me in high school. Other people made similar comments. It's wonderful, but I just wish I had known this back when we were students. I could have used the dose of self-confidence back then.

It is gratifying when people recognize that I am working with a disability. There is a paradox, however. The physically disabled in wheelchairs or with canes and walkers are identifiable. People today largely react supportively to that. I'm not suggesting we hang signs, "Deaf Person," around our necks, but we should inform those with whom we frequently come into contact — store clerks, doormen and neighbors — of our disability.

One of the things that has contributed to my success is a sense of realism. In giving a speech, I like to use the analogy of being a doctor: imagine that if I, as a deaf person, used a stethoscope, anyone I examined would be pronounced dead on arrival. That always gets a laugh; the truth is there are deaf doctors, but anyone going into medicine should have a sense of realism about their specific specialty.

There are limits. King Jordan, the president of Gallaudet, has always said that "deaf people can do anything but hear." There is certainly a lot of truth to this, but there are also some realities.

Can a deaf person be an air-traffic controller? Absolutely, but don't let me be a passenger on the plane he's trying to land. With an interpreter, they can do it, but a three or four second delay could make critical difference, so again, it gets iffy. Again, realism is important.

A sense of humor is important too. I use it a lot. In fact, when I was interviewing for a job, I was facing a committee of four people, seated around a rectangular table. One of the interviewers thought I couldn't see him and asked me if he should move so I could face him and read his lips. It really wasn't a problem, and when he asked, I shot back, asking, "Why? ... Do you need to lip-read?" Everybody cracked up; I hadn't been nervous to start with, but the conversation just snowballed from there. I got the job.

No question about it: Humor really helps. My wit has been one of my hallmarks and one of the keys to my success. It is absolutely essential; if you're disabled and are going to break down the barriers, joking about yourself is a signal to people that you feel okay about yourself.

Interviewing for jobs can be tricky. Another way I have actually used my deafness as an advantage is in not telling a potential employer of my disability. I would prefer that in some cases the interviewer not know that I'm deaf going into the interview; that way, they do find out I'm deaf but only when they meet me. I've applied for jobs for which I've submitted my resume, with all references to deafness eliminated or downplayed; for the Alexander Graham Bell Association for the Deaf, for instance, I put down just "Alexander Graham Bell Association." I wanted them to meet me first because I knew if they did that and then discovered I was deaf, their elevation of respect for me goes up a notch.

I received my cochlear implant in 1990 at the House Ear Institute in Los Angeles. It's made a tremendous difference; I had essentially been without sound for 13 years before that, with my hearing levels dropping steadily on my audiogram. I'm not sure why my hearing had been getting progressively worse; my only thought is that it had declined through a combination of running my hearing aid at the peak and absorbing the noise of the subways back in the early '70s when I was at Columbia and living in New York. Sound improbable? Not really. Those subways are very noisy, and I should have turned my hearing aid off when riding them.

The subways may have been a contributing factor, but we don't know for sure. But I had to stop using the hearing aid because the doctor was afraid that using it could destroy the residual hearing I still had. So he said to wear it only when I really had to hear. That left me essentially without sound and it made me avoid a lot of group situations, because, unless I had an interpreter, I really didn't feel I could function.

That doesn't happen anymore with the implant. Unless a situation is really noisy, I don't mind it; I just have more confidence. Learning to use the implant wasn't difficult; it took a certain amount of auditory training and learning how to listen. And I can now use the telephone and don't have to rely on the operator-assisted relay system. I just pick up the phone — it does have a special connector — dial and talk. It makes a tremendous difference. It's helped me live life to the fullest and helped me look forward to a lot of things in life. I can't wait 'til tomorrow.

Ralph Marra

PLAINVIEW, NEW YORK

You reach Ralph Marra by navigating the canyons of Wall Street, where he is a Vice President in the Securities Services Technology Division of Citibank.

A native New Yorker, Marra incurred a severe, profound hearing loss as a child. His parents, Estelle and Tony, insisted that he attend mainstreamed schools, which he did, earning a B.A. from Fordham University and an M.B.A. from Iona College. He is a longtime volunteer at the League for the Hard of Hearing in New York and a founder and chairman of the League's annual golf outing fundraiser.

Ralph, his wife, Andrea, and their children, Danielle and Anthony, live in Long Island, New York.

One of the first things I remember is when I was in my first or second day of kindergarten near my house in the Bronx section of New York City, when my teacher called on me to go with her to see the principal. We got there and my mother was there, so I immediately knew something was wrong.

I remember my mother asking me why I wasn't listening to the teacher. Here I was — four years old in one of my very first days of school, being asked that question by my mother, the principal and the teacher all being there. It's a very vivid memory; I even remember the teacher's name — Miss Courtney.

The thing is I remember hearing my mother ask me that, which I realized later, because even then, I had probably learned to read lips. But it

Ralph Marra

was an important meeting, because sure enough, Miss Courtney said I wasn't really listening in class. My mother said she couldn't understand it because I was supposedly a real good, polite kid. So, it was shortly after that that my mother took me to get my hearing tested and discovered that I was profoundly deaf.

Was I deaf from birth? I suspect not, because my mother is a very detail-oriented, thorough person who would have picked up something like deafness right away. The last explanation I got was a definition of the cochlea, part of the inner ear, which works like a battery in your ear to filter all the sound. My cochlea never developed, so I suspect it was some kind of degenerative condition. But I don't really care about the explanation for the hearing loss, as long as I'm able to keep what I have.

That's the attitude my parents had. They weren't so much concerned with where the deafness came from, as much as they were with helping me to achieve. I can't say enough about my parents — the fact that I had a hearing problem didn't change their attitude about me. They just kept living a normal way.

That's one of the reasons I was mainstreamed from the beginning. I don't think my parents ever looked at me as a special education student. People would tell them that they ought to consider a special school for me, but they never even considered it. Right away, my mother found the support services of the New York League for the Hard of Hearing, where the philosophy was that as long as I got lip-reading and speech therapy, I could go to a mainstream school.

When I was mainstreamed, my mother insisted that sign language not be used at any time in my lip-reading class at the League for the Hard of Hearing. Today, professionally, I regret it, because there are a lot of opportunities that would come my way if I could sign. I was an adjunct professor for five years at the Bronx branch of Mercy College. I would have liked to participate in a university program for the deaf and hard of hearing. I do plan on doing that someday. Personally, however, I am grateful for not learning sign language at an early age — my speech would not be where it is today if I had done that.

❧

I remember the day I got my hearing aids. It was around the same time that I was diagnosed as being profoundly deaf. I was aided in both ears at the League for the Hard of Hearing. Most vivid is my memory of walking out of the building and up West 23rd Street in Manhattan, holding my dad's hand and turning to him and asking, "What's that?"

It was an airplane. The first time I had ever heard one. I was terrified. Now, West 23rd Street is not really anywhere near an airport — it wasn't landing nearby — so it was pretty high in the air. You could say that my hearing aid picked up pretty well that day.

I was aided in both ears and within days threw off my right aid. My parents looked at me and said, "that didn't last long." The counselors at the League thought I might be getting headaches and some kind of distortion, so her advice was to leave me alone and let me get used to the aids. After awhile, I just got used to one aid — in my left ear — so by the time I got to first grade, I was wearing just the one aid and still do so today.

With my hearing aid, I could hear the teacher in class. Plus, I had started to lip-read by then, and eventually became an expert lip-reader. Today, in fact, I consider myself more than an expert at it — how about a master black belt lip-reader? That's me. When I'm in a crowded restaurant with a lot of noise, I often turn off my hearing aid and just lip-read. A noisy environment would kill the battery in my hearing aid within a half-hour.

❧

Having a handicap, you develop some hidden talents, whether it's a sixth or even a seventh sense. In my case, I really believe that the sense I developed from being deaf has given me the ability to read and figure people out better than most anyone. That means people's motions, gestures, eye contact and the way they speak to you.

I'm convinced that extra sense has helped me be a success in business. When you're deaf, you focus a lot on the face, which tells you a great deal about somebody. You learn to read their face and that's something I've developed over the years. I can sit and read a face and while I might not be able to answer the precise question I'm asked for the first time, I learn a lot about that person.

People without a handicap do not pay enough attention to other people's mannerisms. In business, when I go on an interview, my ability to tap those mannerisms helps me; it tells me something about the person I'm talking with, meaning I already have a head start. When I play baseball, I can automatically tell who on the team I'll be able to communicate with — who will accept my hearing loss and who won't. That, in turn, tells me who will be my friends.

In turn, that ability gives me confidence. I know my limitations, and if I'm with someone and know what kind of person they are from their mannerisms, it helps. If you talk to someone who's blind, this same sense may apply — but with their hearing. In my case, my eyes are my ears. Because of that, I'm successful in a lot of things I've done.

God always blesses handicapped people with that extra sense. If God pre-ordained you to have a handicap, He did so for a reason, and He knows you're a person who can handle it. And if God gave you a child with a handicap, you're very special because He knows you're the kind of parent who can handle that handicap. I really believe that my parents were chosen to take care of a deaf child.

My parents' real contribution was a simple one — they did not treat me any differently than had I not been handicapped, never looked at me as "different" and, in fact, never even used that word. That was the biggest thing: whatever the occasion, they insisted on treating me the same as my brother, five years my junior, and everyone else.

My brother was the same way. Although he had a deaf older brother, he never once, in all the years we shared the same house, did anything to make me feel that I was deaf. Like my parents, he never looked at me as different.

The thing is, I was different. I played baseball from the time I was four years old and never ever with a deaf teammate. I've always been the only one. Even when I was teaching college and went to faculty meetings, I never met another teacher with a hearing aid. Again, always the only one.

That was my family: supportive, always there and aware of the benefit in keeping me in small schools with small classes. I attended Catholic private schools the whole time; it was good for me.

❦

My social life was a different story. That's because kids can be cruel. From the very time I was in kindergarten until my sophomore year in high school, I was the target of bullies; they'd wait outside school for me and pick on me. It didn't help that I was always thin — there were always those three or four bullies who'd want to pick on me. They'd pick on kids because they were thin or nerdy or just different. I was obviously different.

That's one of the reasons I focused on sports. It was something I was good at doing and something where I was accepted. The baseball field was somewhere I could be treated equally. In athletics, even at a young age, if you fit in well and play well, any handicap is overlooked. It was different from being in a classroom or a room full of kids and being the only deaf one there.

How did the bullying affect me? People tell me today that nothing bothers me. They're right to an extent: my attitude is that everything will work itself out, which sometimes drives my wife crazy. "Don't you ever get upset about anything?" she asks me. I think it has a lot to do with the way I was brought up: that no matter how bad things get, you never ever have to stoop to that level, while at the same time, you never think you are better than anyone else.

Even if you feel it, never say you are better than anyone else. I don't feel I am — and I would rather have my actions speak for themselves. That's one of the reasons I have such good longtime friends on whom I can count and call on at anytime.

It didn't happen overnight. I went through a lot of mental anguish, coming home from school, having been picked on that day and afraid to talk about it. I wasn't afraid that my mother would go out and yell at the other kids; I felt that way because I wanted to conquer it myself. I wanted to be mentally strong enough, so that being picked on wouldn't bother me and so I wouldn't go crying to mom.

Today, I do the same thing. If I have a problem at work, for instance, I don't look for someone to complain to, but always try to have things resolve themselves. For me, it works.

In my junior year of high school, things started to get better. That's the year my father always said that my wings flew open. It was the same school — a Catholic private school, which was small. My graduating class was only 85 and the student-to-teacher ratio was 15-to-1, which helped. But a big difference was not having to take the school bus (I had started driving), where I was bullied all the time, just like in grammar school. And I wasn't bullied just because I was deaf; it was in part because I was a freshman — they picked on all the freshmen.

So, my first two years meant taking the bus and staying in my shell. The only thing I did was to join every team I could — I was on the school bowling and baseball teams and played many intramural sports like street hockey and basketball. Actually, I was nervous and afraid to go home on the bus because of the bullies, so I always looked forward to my after-school activity. It meant a lift home from either my mother or someone else's parents.

Then came junior year. What happened is I made the varsity baseball team after two years on the junior varsity team. All the seniors who had gotten on my case for two years suddenly stopped and a few actually became friends. The freshmen and sophomores did not really bother me — hey, I was an upperclassman now. I started to gain the self-confidence that I lacked, and, as my father had said, "My wings flew open."

He was right. I became a student body officer in my junior year and later president of my senior class. I made the Honors Society and even did some light debating on the debate team (that was very short-lived since I never really personally enjoyed that). At Fordham University, I was very involved in student government at the College of Business Administration. In fact I was president in my senior year. In college, I continued to join extracurricular activities because I was accustomed to it after high school. When I look back now, I realize the reason is something a little deeper, and that's where I was successful.

I also realize that like many adventurous people, I tried anything and everything. I think my handicap made me try harder not only for the sake of doing my best, but to prove to myself that I was not limited by my handicap. I even tried water rafting — I went the full journey without a hearing aid, which would be useless if wet, and also meant I didn't hear the guides giving instructions! I just followed what everyone else was doing. Probably the only thing I never cared to try was anything musical because of my hearing problem. To this day, I don't care even when my wife plays music at home. I just have no interest in it.

With one exception, my parents never pushed me in anything. I did it all on my own. The exception was baseball, which my dad helped me with all through my growing up. He always seemed to be my coach — in Little League and summer league, as well as serving as president of the Little League. Baseball was something very close to his heart and it's not that he even pushed me to play; he just was always there for me. There was baseball — and then came everything else.

My high school was all boys, so when I got to Fordham, which, like most all colleges, was coed, I went a little girl crazy. When I was a freshman, I felt I wanted to ask out every girl I met. One girl I remember asking me, over dinner, on our second or third date, "You know why I enjoy going out with you? You pay attention to me and always look at my face." At the time, I had shoulder-length hair, which hid my hearing aid, so she didn't know I was deaf.

It's then I told her that I was actually looking at her face and reading her lips because I was deaf (but only after telling her it was also because she was nice to look at — gotta keep the flattery part in there). It made me realize that eye-to-eye contact was very important, in part, because it gives other people a lot of confidence in you. They can feel you're interested in them, which can be a great advantage in business. That comes naturally to deaf people.

In business, the worst thing for me is trying to listen and talk to somebody who's going through their desk and seemingly doing everything but looking at me. In those situations, I ask them to stop what they're doing for a moment. Most of the time they understand that you may not hear them and they even apologize and correct themselves. But if you think about it, that really has nothing to do with being deaf; it is just common courtesy.

I look back now and I realize that one of the reasons I was successful was that the eye-to-eye contact — i.e., lip-reading — came so naturally. It carries through with everything you do in life; you'll see that people who are successful are generally outgoing and look you right in the eye when they speak to you. People who have something to hide, or are unsure of themselves, tend to face away.

At Fordham, I had a notetaker in class for the first time in my life. I also used a tape recorder, which my mother listened to and would let me know about anything I may have missed in class. If you're deaf, you may have to work harder, but working harder comes a little bit easier. It's not because we don't have the brains, but the brain has to be nurtured — you'll find that many handicapped people work so hard in grammar [school] and high school, that college becomes a snap. We prepare ourselves without knowing it.

Socially, I was worried at first — like every college freshman, I was nervous, but unlike the others, I had one more thing to worry about. To my surprise, things were great — and I had none of the problems I had in high school. In fact, the very first person I met on campus is my best friend today; I was walking across campus on my first day and he was trying to get freshmen to join his fraternity when we met. He was a junior from another part of the Bronx, Co-op City. We struck up a friendship. That was 1976 — more than 25 years ago — and we're still close friends, and so are our wives. I'll mention their names here — Tony and Karen Mascio. I think they'll enjoy seeing their names in this book.

I got my first college job during my junior year, with IBM, which had a student program mandated by law to include people of color and the handicapped. With the help of the League for the Hard of Hearing, I got into the program. It was a work-study program and I went to school three days a week and to work twice a week in New Jersey.

My first job was packing up keypunch cards with rubber bands and making sure I didn't drop them on the way to the computer room. That was the summer of 1978 and I did a host of menial jobs that year. Then, the next summer, before my senior year at college, I started a job involving computer programming. So, in 1980, after I graduated with a double major in finance and managerial accounting and a minor in computers, I got a job at Texaco in White Plains, New York, where I worked until 1983.

There's an important lesson there: I kind of stumbled into computers, largely through a weekend job in the computer room at Fordham and a friendship with the computer professor, who became a kind of mentor. Also, having a father who was a computer programmer was influential. I spent many days as a kid playing with the punch card machines in his office and drawing on the hole-punched computer paper. Today, I really believe that the computer field is one of the fields that offer the best chance for a successful career for a deaf person.

In computer programming, verbal interaction with other people is not the primary task: You interact with the technology that you are using. You rely on your brain and your skills. Sure, meetings and day-to-day people interaction will be a big part of the job, but the career is dependent on the skill-set you have. In contrast, a career like a product manager — where you constantly meet with people and spend hours on the phone — is not exactly the kind of job where a person with a hearing loss can succeed.

In 1983, I was 25 years old and had just gotten engaged to my wife, Andrea, who lived on Long Island. I needed a job that would pay me a better salary, so I learned through an acquaintance about a better paying job on Wall Street with Drexel Burnham Lambert. I landed the job and stayed there until the company folded in 1990. Then, in 1991, my manager from Drexel got a job at Citibank and brought me along. Today, I'm in a managerial role as a Vice President in the Securities Services Technology Division; we're the technology arm for all of the custodial and securities business of the bank.

Deafness is seldom a problem on the job. The only exception is conference calls, and to counter that, I usually have someone attend and take notes for me if I am just listening in. If I am a key person on the call, then I have someone sit next to me and relay the statements to me. After 11 years in the company, most people have come to understand that that is the only way I will be able to handle a conference call.

❧

I love to tell the story about the way I met my wife, Andrea. I was working at Texaco at the time and was invited to a party on Long Island. A friend and I walked into the room where the party was held and a group of women were standing in the corner, talking, laughing and having a good time.

After about 10 minutes, I decided for fun to read their lips and saw they were talking about my friend and me. So I said to him, "watch this." I went over to the girl doing most of the talking and I repeated everything she had said and her jaw dropped open. I was just having some innocent fun. I leveled with her right away — telling her that I was deaf and could read lips. And I told her I was just making a joke as a way of getting to talk to her. The funny thing is the party was on a Friday the 13th, supposedly a bad luck day, while the next day, a Saturday, was Valentine's Day.

To this day, we're not sure when exactly we met — it was either before midnight or after midnight. Anyhow, we started talking, and now, we have been married 17 years and have two children.

I'm still the only deaf person in my family and except for small inconveniences, it's not a hindrance. In all the years growing up, my mother always woke me up. I never had an alarm clock, and besides, my mother was an early bird. I guess that's the way mothers were back then.

So, when I got married, it never occurred to me that Andrea liked to sleep late. I always took it for granted that somebody would wake me up in the morning. It wasn't a problem during our honeymoon, but after we got home and I had to get up early to get to work, it became a problem since I, well, couldn't hear the clock and needed somebody else to wake me up. After a week of that, my wife said, "you know, I'm not your mother."

But we really didn't know of any other way that I could get up myself— that is until we found out about the vibrating alarm clock. The first eight years my wife had to wake me up. For the last nine years though, I've had the vibrating alarm clock, which you put inside your pillowcase and it works by vibrating your pillow; buying it was one of the best things I ever did. It's a great gadget, because that was the only "deaf-related" issue that ever really disturbed her. Otherwise, my deafness is not an issue.

∽

One of the things that really helps me is a sense of humor, and, in particular, my ability to laugh at myself. I got it from my mother and father, who, whenever a joke was made, went along with it. That's something I grew up with — an easy ability to laugh at myself. It is so important for many reasons.

An example: As I got older, I learned to use humor to embarrass the bullies. If a bully sees that his tormenting has no effect on you, then he stops. Taken a step further, if you just laugh or pass off his viciousness, you embarrass the hell out of him. Not only that, but the bully actually learns to respect you, realizing that you're very mature about your handicap. You take the wind out of them.

It even still happens now — in fact, it happened very recently. I play in an age 40-and-up softball league on a team. One of the guys is the resident comedian and always made jokes while I was out of range. It's all friendly, but when I joined the team, I didn't know this guy. A lot of guys laughed and told me not to mind him since he was the team clown. But I went up to him anyway and told him, "Look — I read lips and so I know everything you say." And then I told him that I have a sense of humor about my handicap, and "That if you ever tell any deaf jokes about me and think I will not hear, I guarantee that I will repeat it to you."

He looked at me dumbfounded and apologized, saying he was just kidding around and didn't mean anything. His whole attitude changed. Now, he actually comes over and repeats the joke to me if he thinks I did not catch it! So my motto is to laugh at yourself, but to turn the tables around occasionally. Set some ground rules and never just walk away.

The same thing applies to kids at school. If a bully is picking on you, the father always tells you to be macho and fight back, while your mother tells you not to fight back. What side do you take? What do you do? The bottom line is to stick up for yourself, whether it's punching back, staring someone down or just talking to them. No matter what, don't be afraid to stand up for yourself. No one had to tell me that when I was growing up.

Every school is going to have a couple of kids who will make fun of you if you're handicapped in any way. The way to handle it is be mature about it, use humor if needed and just be accepting of your handicap. It's a lesson worth learning while you're young, because it could be an issue the rest of your life.

I tell kids that because it's something that can help them. Talking to deaf children is something I do as a way of giving back. I do it to help the people of the League for the Hard of Hearing, where I took lip-reading for 11 years, which helped me a great deal.

I realize today that I can't mingle with the deaf community as much as I'd like because I don't know sign language, which bothers me a lot. While I wish I could get involved with deaf kids who are signers, I can't, so helping and communicating with deaf people and children who can lip-read is, in my mind, the next best thing. I suppose it's my way of imparting some of the lessons I learned in growing up.

Helping the League is also my thought in starting the benefit golf tournament. At the time, they had no sports-related benefits, but that can be a great way to raise funds. The tournament started in July 1990, with 26 participants and raised $3,500. By 2000, which was our tenth year, we had 125 golfers and raised $40,000. I view my work with the tournament not only as giving back, but as something I enjoy and something that goes a long way in helping the League provide the quality of services for which they are famous. The League knows what they want to do — they have a target and go after it.

Had you asked me about that in high school, I'd have a completely different answer. It's odd, because I'm a very spontaneous person — getting engaged at a young age and in taking and leaving jobs. I go by gut feeling, not by planning. But as I get older, I start to get more philosophical and look back and appreciate some of the things that have happened to me and why they happened.

That's something I've been trying to remember of late. If you notice, I used some form of the word "handicap" 16 times in this chapter. I never used the word disability. I think that sums up why my life has been so pleasant and successful. The word "disabled" means not being able to function properly. I have been blessed with family, friends, peers and professionals who never made me feel disabled in any way. A handicap is a disability only if it is allowed to be one.

Mildred Oberkotter

PALO ALTO, CALIFORNIA

Mildred Oberkotter has long been active in affairs that benefit the oral deaf community. Her family foundation, started in 1985, has helped hundreds of deaf children attend the schools of their choice. She also volunteers at several schools and for organizations, including the Alexander Graham Bell Association for the Deaf and the Jean Weingarten Peninsula Oral School for the Deaf in Redwood City, California. She received a master's degree from Fordham University and was a social worker for the Lexington Center for Mental Health Services. After living in Long Island and New York City for most of her life, she moved, in 1997, to Palo Alto, California.

I was born in Los Angeles, where my family lived then. My father worked with United Parcel Service, where he started as a clerk and ended up as CEO. But that came much later — a good 40 years later — and, at the time, he was working his way up through the ranks.

To the best of my knowledge, I was born hearing, and became deafened from a high fever from influenza when I was eight months old. I recovered from the illness, but I'm pretty sure I lost my hearing in the process.

My mother suspected I wasn't hearing anything and took me to several doctors, who said I was fine. Still, she suspected and continued her visits to doctors. Eventually, she found one who confirmed her suspicions and I was diagnosed as profoundly deaf at the age of one and a half. In those days, it was thought that placing a hearing aid on a small child would ruin what little residual hearing that child had, so it just wasn't done.

So, I have to hand it to my mother. She would put me on her lap, place my hands on her mouth and talk and talk to me. It's how I developed my speech-reading skills. She used a great deal of common sense in trying to help me — and she did.

My mother came through again after we'd moved to Philadelphia (when I was three), finding an ad in *The Volta Review* for a small school for deaf children near home. It was the start of formal speech therapy and group work and play for me; there were 10 to 15 students in the school, all of us in one classroom.

I was the only student who lived at home; the rest were boarders. It just goes to show how my parents had become advocates for me when I was still very young. You like to think that every parent becomes an advocate for their children, but my parents, as with most parents of handicapped children, assumed that role much earlier than most.

My father was transferred once again, to New York City, when I was six years old and ready for first grade. My parents shopped around for an appropriate school for me in the area; it was a school visit that became the turning point for me as far as my education went.

✧

There, following the testing session, the interviewer reported to my parents that I was "too oral" for a deaf school. Then, she recommended we consider a school in Port Washington, Long Island, started by the mother of a deaf boy. This mother had the vision of a school for both the deaf and those who could hear, and when my mom visited the school, she became enraptured with the place. So, we moved to Manhasset, Long Island, to be close to the school.

I went there for my first eight years of elementary school. On its staff, there was always a trained teacher for the oral deaf. Typically, I was pulled out of class for about an hour each day for one-on-one speech/language/ remedial work. Otherwise, I was completely integrated in the regular classroom with no other support, other than to make the teacher aware of my classroom needs. The boy whose mother had begun the school and I were the only two oral deaf students who continued at the school for the full eight years.

Over the years, some hearing children who needed special help joined the program for a year or two. All the other children had normal hearing, and I always felt I was a part of this environment and thrived as a result. The school was a cooperative one, meaning parents of the students were expected to help out in various ways to cut down on costs. That's how my parents interacted with the other parents and staff members.

Another of the school's special features was its progressive nature. It was like the little red schoolhouse, where classes were composed of two or three grades each. Here's how it worked: while the classroom teacher worked with students from one grade, students from the other grades worked with and helped one another. I had strong arithmetic skills, so I helped some of the other students with their math, while others helped me with my written language and grammar.

Mildred Oberkotter

We learned to work together and support one another. Those were happy years for me; I had friends among my classmates. Time outside the classroom was spent playing with the many children in the neighborhood; chief among them, a very special "chum" who lived in back of my house — we were inseparable.

I also tagged along with my older brother and his playmates and did many and great mischievous things with them. At that point, I didn't feel different from any of the others; I sort of identified myself with my parents and my brother who is three-and-a-half years older than me. They were all reserved and reticent. I was made to feel a part of this environment in spite of my being the only deaf child in the family and in the neighborhood.

There was something very valuable that was instilled in me in those days: an inner sense of confidence that served me well then and continues to do so today. Basically, I had pretty much a normal childhood, where I was allowed to be a child, except when I had to go for speech and language training, which was something the others didn't have to do. I can't stress enough how ordinary it all was. That's important for parents of hard of hearing children to know — there should be time for their kids to have fun and feel a part of their worlds.

❧

Things started getting difficult when I was around 12 years old. That's when I became an adolescent with an identity crisis. On top of it all, my chum moved away from the neighborhood, meaning I was separated from my closest friend and confidante of the previous six years. In a nutshell, I became aware that I was "different" the first time I encountered difficulty in getting the kids to understand what I was saying. Rather than persist, I retreated to my home, read books and pursued hobbies.

I finally got a hearing aid when I was 14. I didn't wear it much, and, in hindsight, it would have helped me. About the only time I seemed to wear it was going to the movies; otherwise, I put it away a lot, because I was just very self-conscious. It was that time I was ready for high school, but the local public school was reluctant to enroll me.

The result is that I went away to high school — Oakwood School in Poughkeepsie, NY. It would be my first time away from home. I remember my mother warning me that "some" people would be uncomfortable with me and recommending that I be prepared with a pad of paper and pencil to facilitate the communication process. My reaction was a natural one for someone of that age who was reserved and self-conscious; I reasoned that my mother's "some" meant "everyone." So, I withdrew and just didn't talk very much.

It wasn't all gloom and doom. I learned a lot at Oakwood; in class, I sat in the front row and lipread the teachers. I also sat next to fellow students who took notes of what I hoped was the teacher's most important points. And when I had questions or felt I missed something in class, I'd usually go to the teachers after class or did extra reading to enhance my understanding of the subjects.

All those things helped, and in time, I coped and did pretty well academically. Besides, I worked twice as hard as anyone else in school, which is a given when you're deaf. It all worked, so much so that I had some fun in class. Oddly, one of the things that sticks out most in my mind about those days in school is that sometimes the classes got boring — yes, boring — and I'd spend some of my time, passing lessons as well as personal notes back and forth with my seat mates. That was fun. Classes were small, about 20 to a room. However, the individualized attention and smaller classes were the reasons my parents sent me to Oakwood. It paid off.

❧

Sports became my social outlet. I played field hockey, basketball and softball, in part because it was just plain fun, and, in part, because I was just another athlete on the playing field, and not treated any differently. In sports, you're picked because of your talent and not out of pity; I liked that, I was good at it, and sports gave me a lot of self-confidence at the time when I could really use it. It was great to know that I was a contributor and could be treated like anyone else.

Besides, I had really started to find myself by then. My self-confidence continued to grow; I had just decided for myself that I was going to have to grow up and get along if I was going to get anywhere.

There was another factor to my gaining self-confidence — my roommate at Oakwood. She and I just communicated really well with one another and developed a strong friendship, which meant a lot to me. At the time, I had a loud voice — that can happen when you're deaf, young and not wearing hearing aids. My roommate once told me that some of the fellow dorm mates could hear me through the thin walls and understand me. That was hard for me to believe, considering my perception of what my mom told me just before I started high school. My inherent reserve and reticence got in the way and helped me through.

I graduated from Oakwood in 1953 and enrolled at Green Mountain College, a two-year college for women in Vermont as an Accounting/Business Administration major. I lived in a small dorm — there were 50 women in this dorm — and continued to find myself socially. Again, I had an outlet, which, in this case, was the group card game and bridge. The dorm had a lounge, or what we called a "smoking room" back then, and the major activity there was bridge.

Through that, I became an avid bridge player and fit right in. As in high school, I was never a part of any cliques, but I did okay both socially and academically; in both places, I had friends, but not a lot. You don't need a lot of friends, nor do you have to be part of a clique or a gang. It took me a long time to realize that, but it's true.

I graduated from Green Mountain in 1955 and moved back home to Manhasset, where I commuted to a job in Manhattan. Keep in mind that this was the '50s — well before the Women's Movement of the '60s — and women in their early 20s, like me at the time, didn't generally live on their own.

My first job was in sales and it was in that job that I enjoyed interacting with my co-workers. It was also around then that I became actively involved in golf, a game that I had learned when I was 16. I spent quite a bit of time at golf, going so far as to play in tournaments.

And it was around then when I heard from my old deaf schoolmate from Port Washington. He had found out about a club for oral deaf young adults and encouraged me to attend one of their meetings. At the same time, I also got in touch with an old classmate from the pre-school in Philadelphia — a young woman living in New York at the time — and we resumed that friendship. So, there I was with two renewed friendships, right off the bat. That marked my introduction into the deaf environment.

The club was called "The Merry Go-Rounders." It had about 150 members — people of all kinds and from all walks of life — and it became a wonderful outlet. For the first time in my life, I was with a group of oral deaf people with whom I felt comfortable. We socialized, and, as deaf people, we were all in the same boat, so no club member ever felt left out or any different. I even met my husband, Ed, through the "Merry Go-Rounders." We married in 1964, when I was 29 and we were married for 24 years, divorcing in 1988.

My husband and I moved into Manhattan, living on the Upper East Side for six years, and then on the Upper West Side for most of our marriage. Along the way, I made a career change, becoming, in 1972, a computer programmer. It was the dawn of the computer age and computers intrigued me. Looking back, I can't think of a better career choice for deaf and hard-of-hearing people at the time: In that early period of commercial computers, you weren't dependent on your hearing, which put you on a level playing field — there's that analogy again — with everyone else.

In a more general sense, I realize that I've been very lucky in the support I received growing up as well as in the choices I've made as an adult. Yes, I'm proud of myself, but I also think it's very important to give back. I was lucky and I just want to help others get some of the same breaks that I got as a child. That's why I volunteered as a teacher's aide at a local school for the deaf, worked as a therapist at a physical rehabilitation center and served on various committees.

That's the reason, as well, for the foundation — the Oberkotter Foundation — that my parents started in 1985. We have two primary missions: helping people suffering from diabetes; and, the other, helping oral deaf children succeed in appropriate educational settings that can allow these children to achieve personal fulfillment, happiness and their aspirations.

I know that parents of hearing impaired children have some hard choices to make at a time when mainstreaming in public schools can sometimes be inappropriate for deaf and hard of hearing students. This means there are a lot of times when parents have to either take it or leave it.

In today's world where both parents have to work just to make ends meet, many families find themselves needing financial help if they aim to send their child to a private school. I know the advantages of private schools for some deaf children — the smaller classes and individualized attention can be real pluses — and I want to make it easier for parents who want to send their hearing-impaired children to a private school. So, with the support of the Alexander Graham Bell Association for the Deaf in Washington, D.C., our Foundation has made it possible to send hundreds of children over the years to private schools, pre-school through high school. Yes, this is my way of giving back.

Part of my desire to give back was another personal choice involving a further career change in the late 1980s. I decided to go back to complete my undergraduate studies, getting a B.A. in psychology and then to become certified as a social worker. I had discovered that I really enjoyed working with people and this afforded me the chance to do that. I got my degree — a master's in social work — from Fordham University in 1991.

I decided to specialize in working with deaf and hard of hearing youngsters at the Lexington School for the Deaf in New York, which also required that I learn to sign. I stayed at Lexington for five years, before retiring in 1995; then, in 1997, after more than 40 years in New York, I decided to make another change, this time moving to Palo Alto. I still get back to New York frequently, and my goodness, it's so noisy and dirty. I guess I'm becoming a laid-back Californian, after all!

Moving away from where I lived so long makes one reflective. Was I fortunate? Yes, I've had a good life. Would I have done it any differently? That can be answered several ways. On one hand, growing up, there's something I clearly would have done differently: I think it would have been great to have had a deaf role model, somebody to go to or look up to who would have understood what I was going through when I was growing up. Oh, I had friends, but not the peer support that I could have used.

On the other hand, I'm happy I'm oral; I prefer to speak rather than sign. I know my speech isn't perfect, but it's okay. The way I look at it is by speaking and signing, I have the best of both worlds.

George Oberlander, Jr.

HARRISON, NEW YORK

George Oberlander, Jr., is the recipient of The League for the Hard of Hearing's 1997 Personal Achievement Award. A graduate of Hofstra University and a director with Syska & Hennessy Engineers in New York City, Oberlander was honored, in part, for his work as a mentor with the League's Career Development Department and for being a frequent motivational speaker to parents of hearing-impaired youngsters.

I have been deaf since birth, but remained undiagnosed until almost kindergarten. Most people would probably think it was a disadvantage to be diagnosed so late. I believe the reason I lip-read so well is I had to rely on this means as my only form of communication during those early years. Some time ago, *The New York Times* ran an article about my special education teacher. The reporter later told me her editor didn't believe it had taken so long for me to be diagnosed. What can I say? Doctors back then didn't have the expertise they have today. They figured the reason I didn't seem to be hearing was because I was a daydreamer. Also, I had no older siblings talking to me.

I have a severe to profound bi-lateral sensorial hearing loss. Normal hearing allows frequencies up to 8,000Hz to be heard at 20db. I do not hear frequencies above 1,000Hz, even when amplified with a hearing aid to 110db. This is similar in volume to a jet engine. It is like trying to hear on a moving subway train. Also, I do not hear particular sounds such as "sh" and "ph" among others.

George Oberlander

I don't remember a great deal about life before the hearing aids. My mother tells me I had trouble with my speech but otherwise I was a "normal" child. Her suspicions began to grow when, while she was talking out the kitchen window with her back to me, I said "Mom, please turn around, I can't see what you're saying." Her doubts grew even more when she was reading a book to me called *The Little Engine That Could.* A major line from the book comes when the blue engine says to himself as he was trying to pull the cars over the mountain: "I think I can, I think I can, I think I can." When I tried to repeat the same line from the book, I would pronounce it "ack a dunde, acka dunde, ack a dunde."

I remember that book very well, not only because of my lifelong love for model railroading, but also because, as a kid who unknowingly had a disability, it helped heighten the self doubts that were emerging. There is a lot of truth that what you learn and what you experience in your early years affects you for the rest of your life, or habits formed early in life are deeply implanted.

I received my first hearing aid when I was five years old and thought it was the coolest looking thing in the world. I remember being in the car on the way home after getting it and thinking that the new sounds that it was bringing to me were no big deal; it was a toy to me.

My mother tells me that it took a few months for me to adjust to the new hearing aids. I was constantly taking them off. Most new hearing aid wearers make the mistake of thinking it's like putting on and taking off a pair of glasses. Believe me, it takes time to adjust; it's similar to learning a new language because the sounds are so different from what you're used to, especially if you've never heard a distinct sound before.

Recently, I saw an interview on television with a deaf woman who said she thought it was better to be deaf than hearing because it focuses you. But I can tell you that when I first put on my hearing aid in the morning the world comes alive. There are no words to describe the feeling. I don't mind, however, not being able to hear when I'm sleeping. I always tell anyone who is trying on new hearing aids that it's a good idea to give it a few months before making a decision about whether it is helping. It takes some people longer then others to get used to them. Don't give up too early.

Somehow, my mother knew that I had to be patient. So, to help me with getting used to the hearing aid, she suggested that I just wear them only when watching television. Up until then, I was used to reading lips. Now, I had a whole new dimension added to my ability to receive and communicate, and I suspect that it took time for me to learn how to use these new tools that were given to me.

It took a few months of wearing the hearing aids to achieve a comfort level, and I wore them most of the time after that. Today, I put them on when I get up and do not take them off until I go to bed. In fact, I'm very uncomfortable when I'm not able to hear, especially when there is a lot of activity or people around me. Both as a child and today, I wear two body aids because they help me the most. Because my hearing is so poor, I need the extra power that body aids provide.

Some people wear behind-the-ear units because they look better cosmetically, and they also believe that their hearing aids are powerful enough for them to hear well. I've tried to wear behind the ear units, even the new programmable ones. However, I find that the body aids I wear offer trouble-free clear sound for me, both in person-to-person communication and on the telephone. Every once in a while I will try out the latest hearing aids to see if they improve my ability to communicate. I have found that the latest hearing aids are very good for listening in a crowded environment, but they do not allow me to hear well on the phone, therefore I wear the behind-the-ear for social events, where there is background noise, and my body aids for work, where I spend a lot of time on the phone.

I found that being able to communicate without a hearing aid required more then just being able to lip-read well. It also included being able to anticipate what the other person was saying and obtaining information via body language and situations. For example, when my mother was talking to me and looking out the window, obviously I didn't hear her. I probably saw that her jaw was moving and determined that she was talking to me. I would say that more than 50 percent of comprehending day-to-day communication comes from anticipating what the other person is about to say. Many times someone will walk up to me in the office and I'll answer their question before they have had a chance to ask it. They usually walk away shaking their head, probably thinking "how'd he do that?" (I have been doing this for more than 30 years).

I received my hearing aids about three months before the start of kindergarten and consequentially became more aware of my difficulty in enunciating words, especially my own last name, which is more then a bit of a tongue twister. I remember not wanting to go to school on the first day of first grade because "I didn't know my Oberlander."

Once I got used to the hearing aids, the next step was the telephone. Here was an example of "can't do that." At first, my mother told my friends who called that I couldn't speak on the telephone and she'd take a message. But when I was about seven or eight, one day I decided on my own to try to use the phone. At first, I had difficulty. I asked my mother for help, but eventually, by trial and error and practice I gradually became proficient at using the phone. It was like that with a lot of things. My parents were instrumental in helping me develop a "can do" attitude, which comes, in part, from never hearing them mention can't, couldn't or shouldn't do that.

An example of "Shouldn't be doing that?" Using a walkie-talkie as a kid. Growing up, my friends and I played a game of war in which we chose teams, staked out boundaries and then tried to shoot the members on the other team before they shot you. Each team was equipped with a walkie-talkie so they could coordinate. The team shooting all the members of the other team won the game.

As the deaf kid, I faced immediate challenges. First, how would I know I had been shot? Second, how could I hear on the walkie-talkie? I didn't always know that I had been shot, since I couldn't hear on the walkie-talkie. But I was able to play along because we played in teams. Basically, I relied on my teammates to listen and then to tell me what was happening. My mother said it best: "When my friends ran, I ran. When they stopped, I stopped." It was a case of using their senses to supplement my own. Little did I know then that I was developing skills that would eventually help me function in the hearing world.

Between the ages of five and 12, the kids in the neighborhood and at school picked on me. They did it because I was different. It's part of the package that many deaf, handicapped and normal children go through; and if you have experienced it and can get through it, you definitely come out a stronger person. People ask me if I resented my friends who picked on me. I tell them that kids will be kids, and nothing will change that.

There were times — lots of times — when I'd go out to play, only to come back into the house and complain to my mother that the other kids were picking on me. After comforting me, she would just turn me around and send me back out, telling me to stand up for myself. The same thing happened at school. I'd come home complaining that the kids were picking on me, and she'd tell me to go back and deal with it. I also remember my grandfather, who lived with us in an upstairs apartment, telling me to fight back when kids picked on me.

It was my dad who made sure that my childhood was not all work and no play. He took his own enjoyment of model airplanes and trains to help create a diversion from my frustrations with school. In fact, one of his best and most famous diversions was the creation of a neighborhood airplane club for the kids. He'd pile us into his station wagon, drive us to a local field and give everybody the opportunity to fly an airplane. My dad even picked up the tab for gas for each plane, and once in awhile he would pile us all into the car again and take everybody to airplane shows. In doing so, he gave me a reputation, not as the deaf kid, but as the one with the cool dad who took everyone flying. My friends even designated me as the best flyer in the club, which did a lot for my self-esteem; and in retrospect, they were not stupid.

It was the same with model railroading. Once again, my dad took charge by building a train set in our basement where my friends and I spent a lot of time. Some parents may cringe at the thought of a house full of kids, but my parents welcomed it: They had an open door policy in which the neighborhood kids came and went at will. For me, it made things a whole lot easier. It helped me forget my frustrations and just focus on having fun.

Whenever I talk to my childhood friends, they always remember my father with great fondness. Some even say he was like a second father to them, because their own dads were always working. One of them thanked my father right before he died for helping to choose his career. Today, he's a pilot for a major airline.

My father was always available and accessible. I knew exactly what time he'd pull into the driveway after work — 5:10 P.M. on the button. And I'm saddened that many children today, both disabled and non-disabled, live in a society in which parents have to work so hard to make ends meet that they have very little time with their children.

An important point for parents of hearing-impaired youngsters to remember is that there is no way siblings can or will ever get the same attention as the handicapped child. It's just not possible. In my family I have a sister who is two years younger, which could have been difficult, except for the fact that she did well in school and wasn't dependent on my parents to the same extent that I was.

I emphasize to parents of handicapped children to be aware of potential problems of siblings and to try to balance their attention as much as possible. A normal sibling relationship is difficult enough to handle, but the relationship between a handicapped child, non-handicapped children and the parents is especially difficult. There's no way you can give each child equal attention; a handicapped child always requires more energy, attention, patience and, most importantly, time.

For parents of a hearing-impaired child, I find the biggest secret to success is letting your kids be normal as often as possible. The tendency is to take them from speech therapy to special education class and be overly protective. But my parents were never afraid to let me go out and play with the other kids in the neighborhood. They just let me mess up like a regular kid and learn and grow in the process.

It was the Harrison School system that eventually diagnosed that my speech impediment was caused by a hearing deficiency. As part of the evaluation process I had been sent to Irwin Rickler, a speech therapist who worked for the school system. Mr. Rickler's evaluation confirmed what my mother already suspected, that I had a hearing problem.

At that point, he called my pediatrician and asked him to find someone reputable and qualified to diagnose the condition professionally. I went to Westchester County Medical Center where I was given a series of hearing tests and eventually diagnosed with a severe-to-profound hearing loss. Remember, back in the '60s, there were no textbooks to describe how to handle a child who had just been diagnosed as hearing impaired. Instead of automatically sending me off to a school for the deaf, which was done in most cases like mine, they decided that I should be mainstreamed.

In fourth grade, partly in response to problems I was having, such as inventing psychosomatic illnesses to avoid going to gym class and partly in response to not keeping up in my studies, the Harrison School District decided to take some action. My homeroom teacher was concerned I wasn't responding or keeping up in class, especially when she was at the blackboard or walking across the room.

In response, the school system looked into purchasing the Travel EarTM, an early version of the FM unit enjoyed by hard-of-hearing children today.

The Harrison School District wasn't ready to exercise the school for the deaf option just yet. The Travel Ear involved the teacher wearing a microphone and I would wear a receiver that would pump the teacher's voice directly into my ear without any background noise. The device opened my "ears" to the world around me. Looking back, I'm fortunate the Harrison School District explored all the available options, and they did it in the days before the Americans with Disabilities Act (ADA). Without knowing it, the District was helping to pave new roads for other handicapped children to enter into the mainstream.

In fifth grade, I had a teacher who never thought I'd make it through middle school or high school and she thought I should enroll at the New York School for the Deaf. My mother argued strongly against that option by using report cards showing I'd done well in previous grades. My mother could have taken me out of that class, but she didn't. Her attitude was I had to learn how to deal with all kinds of adversity. It was tough, but it paid off. That was the closest that I ever came to going to a school for the deaf, during my K–12 years.

In sixth grade, the Harrison School District provided me with my first tutor. Until then, I had relied on my teachers and my mother to "fill in the blanks." Most of the teachers encouraged me and believed that I could succeed. And so I got together again with Mr. Rickler, who worked with me three time a week on vocabulary development and articulation.

There were some other things that my parents arranged at school to help me. I was able to sit in the front row and they instructed my teachers that they should face the class — not the blackboard when speaking — so I could hear and lip-read. But mostly, it was up to me. For example, in my first few days of first grade, I raised my hand and told the teacher I couldn't hear what she was saying. That teacher told my mother later that she couldn't believe a 6 year old kid could have the presence of mind to do something like that.

In general, I didn't like school very much. I wanted to play rather then do my homework. In hindsight, that wasn't very wise, because if you're deaf, you have to work harder then others to get ahead. Eventually, I realized I'd better work harder. As part of my change in attitude, I went from poor attendance in elementary school to perfect attendance in high school and college.

My special ed teacher "filled in the blanks." On average, I'd spend an hour a day with her and we covered many questions on many subjects. Looking back, I'm amazed at how many different things we covered in math, science, English and history. My special education teacher never made any excuses about doing any tasks or covering any subject. If she didn't know the answer, we would work together to solve the problem. That's another secret for success — never make excuses, and ask for help when you need it!

∾

Social life in elementary school consisted of playing sports, both at school and home. I noticed that when I played with a group of kids, I was considered different. But playing with one of my friends one-on-one, the disability was less noticeable and I was just like everyone else. Why? I think the difference is that kids tend to jockey for position and status in group situations. I remember being mad at them for having a double standard. But looking back, I accept it today as the way kids behave. It had nothing to do with my being deaf, but more because I was different. In the long run, dealing with being teased and then understanding their attitude made me a better stronger person.

In both middle school and high school, I was fortunate because the school district realized that for me to succeed in a mainstream setting, I'd need more support then I received in elementary school. So they assigned a teacher of the deaf to work with me every day to fill in the information that I missed in class, and to help my teachers make modifications to the classroom environment. This resource teacher not only filled in the blanks, but gave me the skill and confidence to speak in front of people.

As I grew older, life moved away from playing sports to more social interactions like dances and parties. At the same time that it became easier for me to play sports with a group of people, it became harder for me to keep up with the social crowd. I spent much of my spare time in wood-working and power mechanics shop. I enjoyed working with mechanical things and spent much of my high school years doing just that.

Since then, I have come to realize that certain types of socializing can be overrated. When I was in my 20s, I'd go out to a bar with my friends after working late at a local McDonald's. One night, just outside the bar, someone grabbed my head from behind and smashed me into a parked car, knocking my hearing aid into the sewer. I remember asking myself, "What am I doing?" And I remember thinking that this social "thing" is not all it's cracked up to be. The fact that I can spend my time rebuilding a car, work-ing on my train set, or renovating the back porch of my house, all of which I enjoy immensely, can be just as good use of my time as going out to a bar. The downside is it withdraws you from more social interaction.

In high school I didn't socialize that much, but spent a lot of time working on cars and building things with wood. The important thing is to have the self-confidence to do what you want to do. If some people like going to bars, great. But I'd rather do something else. When, for instance, I'm working on my car or in the shop, I'm having the time of my life. When I was a kid, if there was something mechanical, look out; I'd fix it. I'd also spend many hours taking things apart and putting them back together just to learn how they worked.

◈

That mechanical aptitude was a good start to my becoming an engineer. I remember taking a fifth grade aptitude test in which I said that I wanted to become an electrical engineer. I just always liked to build and design things; it was that simple. And since I always aimed for a professional career, it made sense. When you are deaf, you have to be realistic; after all there are a number of careers that I just didn't consider, like being a telephone operator or a salesperson. At the time, I felt that I had to avoid jobs that required excessive communication and using the telephone.

During middle school and high school, I considered attending college at Rochester Institute of Technology (RIT). I visited the campus twice — once during the seventh grade, and later, in the tenth grade. My special education teacher even came along on the second trip. I remember the school guide saying that to attend RIT, I'd have to spend my first two years at the National Technical Institute for the Deaf (NTID) to learn sign language before enrolling in RIT. "Wait a minute," I remember asking the campus tour guide, "I can speak ... I've been mainstreamed all my life and now you want me to spend two years learning to sign?" I didn't want that. So in the end, I decided not to attend RIT.

Then, my special education teacher told me about Hofstra University on Long Island that specialized in accepting applicants with disabilities. Keep in mind that my combined SAT score of 900 (350 verbal and 550 math) didn't meet the minimum required (1,100) to enter Hofstra's regular curriculum. So my parents, special education teacher and I met with Dean Spencer, who was in charge of Hofstra's handicapped program. Because of Hofstra's extensive experience with the handicapped, Dean Spencer decided to accept me into the engineering curriculum, but only if I would agree to try their "New College" program for the first semester.

New College was a special program created by Hofstra to give applicants who did not perform well in high school, but had good potential, a chance to get a college diploma. So, I accepted the offer to go there, did very well and after the first semester, was accepted into the university's regular engineering program.

Because of Hofstra's work with the disabled, and I suspect for insurance reasons as well, I was housed on a handicapped floor of the dorm. I was even paired up with a paraplegic roommate, who had recently broken his neck after diving at the beach. Other students on the floor had various types of disabilities: multiple sclerosis, blindness, ALS (Lou Gehrig's disease), spina bifida, and severed limbs among others. Some nonhandicapped students were also on the floor and I remember a friend visiting me and saying, "It's like living in a hospital." In some ways, she was right; it was definitely a unique living environment.

My first reaction when I found out that I would be living in this type of environment was "Where the heck are they putting me?" It took a long time for me to get used to the idea of living in this environment. Eventually, the disabilities began to disappear and the individual personalities began to emerge. So instead of the first impressions such as "He's the guy with no legs" or "He's the blind guy" and "There goes the paralyzed guy," the people on my floor became "The guy I liked to wrestle with" and "The guy with a dog" and "The guy who likes the Yankees." I even wrestled with my roommate, despite his severe disability.

That was all part of a pattern. Each year, when new "handicapped" persons moved onto the floor, I'd find myself focused on their disabilities, and then their personalities. I thought to myself that this must be part of the friction that exists between people who are different. I noticed that the personalities of each individual helped me (or not) to shift from my initial focus on their disability to the person behind the disability. I quickly relaxed with people who were comfortable with their disabilities and were willing to educate me about their individual situations. Others weren't so comfortable, making it difficult for me to see past their personal challenges.

New College was easy. It was like going back to high school. On weekends, I picked up extra spending money by working at McDonald's, and I thought I'd be able to continue working there during the second semester. But the honeymoon lasted only two weeks into the engineering program: It's then I realized that engineering was difficult, really difficult; and to keep up, I had to give up the McDonald's job, as well as another job I had on campus. I even stopped going home weekends, because all of a sudden, I needed the time to study. Just like that, I was working harder than I ever had in my life. But I had no problem with working hard because I wanted that engineering degree in the worst way.

Even so, I got Cs and Ds in my first semester of engineering, which was downhill big time from high school. Not only did I have to work harder then the other students because I was deaf, but engineering itself is a tough major, plain and simple. The engineering program was the kind of major that a lot of people would start, but eventually quit. They'd find they just couldn't hack it and move onto something else.

In high school, I had a solid support network from my family, friends and the special ed teacher, all of which I didn't have at college. Losing that hometown network was difficult: College meant a total change, including having to build up a whole new group of friends. And in the engineering program, you have to really, really want that degree. So I knew I'd have to make a new set of friends and build a new support system. It took time, but eventually I began adjusting, made a "comeback" and thrived. But it wouldn't have happened had I not been persistent, determined and strong willed as my mother had been earlier on.

But even persistent, determined and strong-willed people need a break once in a while. This break came in the form of Paul Falvey, a surrogate father. Mr. Falvey was a friend of my roommate and would visit us every so often, usually with a beer for my roommate and a soda for me. Seeing that I worked so hard, Mr. Falvey would force me to get away from it by taking me to hockey games at the Nassau Coliseum on Tuesday night and swimming on Thursday nights, when there were no tests of course. As I look back on my college experience, it becomes clear that these nights out were the only real relief I got from my struggles to become an engineer.

My college experience can be described in three words: "work, work and work." I wasn't provided with tutors, but I did get paid note takers from the Office of Vocational Rehabilitation. Because I had taken my own notes in high school, I found it hard to use other people's notes. But, I was able to adjust: whereas in high school, notes were written on the blackboard and you could recopy them into your notebook, college meant sitting in the classroom just trying to absorb the content of the teacher's lecture. Because I was spending so much time trying to understand the words, it was hard for me to comprehend what they meant. As a result, my comprehension in the classroom wasn't very good, which I made up for by studying very long hours using the notes.

I remember taking an introductory engineering course, when a guy sitting next to me in class turned and said, "I don't know if I'll like engineering, but I'm going to try it." I remember thinking to myself that I wouldn't be seeing him the following semester, and I didn't. Sure they made adjustments for me at Hofstra — the New York State Office of Vocational Rehabilitation provided a note taker and New College really did help — but the bottom line was I still had to get the grades. There were no concessions or grade inflations on tests. I wouldn't have wanted it any other way.

To put things into perspective, I remember asking a bunch of guys what they did on Friday nights. Their typical response was "I went out with my friends." Then, I'd tell them that on Friday nights, I did my engineering lab reports.

The biggest help came from the engineering professors, who would give me all of the office time I needed and never made me feel that I was out of place or that I was imposing. Later, one professor called me his "best customer." I would probably have never made it without their help.

One of my proudest accomplishments is graduating from Hofstra with my engineering degree. Getting that degree was a goal I remember setting for myself in seventh grade and I never allowed myself to stray from that goal. When I finally got my diploma, all the frustrations, late study nights, failures, emotional highs and lows, and successes had paid off.

Today, I'm always sure to recommend engineering as a course of study to deaf students, but only if their math scores are solid and they feel that they will enjoy it. With engineering, you don't have to worry whether your English, history or foreign language scores are great; although I still tell my younger cousins and the students I mentor that it is essential you learn to write well, since our society demands it. You must be able to communicate.

I received my long-awaited engineering degree from Hofstra University in May of 1985. Just before graduating, I called the League for the Hard of Hearing and the International Center for the Disabled, both in New York City, to ask about engineering job leads. Both organizations provided some guidance in résumé writing and interview training, and even secured some interviews with various large companies. My anxieties were relieved however when I landed an interview with Syska & Hennessy through the typical networking trail.

To say that upon my graduation, I was a confident person with no fear of working in the hearing world would be a gross overstatement. I had great anxieties about functioning in the hearing environment, especially using the telephone. At the time, the phone was my biggest fear. "How am I going to handle it?" I recall asking myself. But looking back, it hasn't really been a problem for all practical purposes.

Sure, there are times when someone calls me and I can't follow the conversation that well. It happened recently, when the person calling me was a stranger and the conversation was awkward in the beginning. In that situation; it took a few minutes, but like most of the time, I caught on. You pick up little tricks along the way, like guessing what the person will say before they say it. Believe it or not this is one of my best tricks although I think some of my coworkers will say that it is annoying. Most of them understand it is part of how I communicate but I realize that others may perceive it that I am not a good listener.

How can you be a good listener if you cannot hear? I need this and other tricks in order to communicate in the hearing world. Without them, I would not be able to function as well as I do. The annoying part of this trick is that, when I guess wrong, it frustrates that talker. I constantly look for ways to improve my "listening" skills, but in the end there is always a compromise between being a good listener and using the tricks.

My hopes were realized when Syska & Hennessy called me for an interview. This was a great opportunity — they're a U.S.-wide top-of-the-line engineering firm that specializes in mechanical, electrical and plumbing projects and employ more than 600 people. I wanted the job in the worst way.

Jack Presad, who wasn't born in the U.S and had an accent, interviewed me. I had a great deal of difficulty understanding him. The interview didn't go as well as I had hoped and I didn't think I'd be called back for a second interview. But, as it turned out, he was impressed with my summer work experience with IBM as a Maintenance Engineer, so he forwarded my resume to Mark Davidson, the company's Vice President of the Facilities Management Division.

Mr. Davidson also wasn't easy for me to understand because he spoke very fast. But something must have triggered him to try something different: Instead of talking to me about new and strange engineering topics, he steered the conversation to personal interests I had listed in my resume under "activities" — restoring cars and skiing. When I discovered that he enjoyed the very same interests, I was elated and relaxed. He later told me that as soon as we got to topics I was familiar with, the conversation flowed smoothly and he got a good feeling for my personality and qualifications.

I was hired, but there was one condition: if it does not work out for whatever reason, we will have to let you go. In the end Mr. Davidson was tough but fair. It worked out.

I had finally reached my goal: a position with a well-known, highly-respected engineering firm as an engineer-in-training. A vice president had decided to take a chance, but leveled with me from the start by saying that my disability could not interfere with my job accomplishments. I had to perform up to their standards. As a person who likes to be on the level, I didn't have a problem with that.

So, I worked for the Facilities Management Division for six years, where I learned about AutoCAD, a computer software program that allows engineers to create drawings, building maintenance and building systems. Each passing day, my confidence about functioning in a hearing environment grew.

At the same time, I can say that it never gets easier. Some people do not enunciate particularly well on the phone or get annoyed when I ask them to repeat something. I try to not answer their calls directly and have a secretary take the messages. These are some of the tricks of the trade that I use. I have learned to shrug this off and work harder.

Some people resented what they perceive as my getting special treatment by some teachers or bosses some of the time. Some even said that I was trying to be a teacher's pet, and so forth. If you can't convince them otherwise just shrug it off and go on.

At times, I was floundering and had difficulty relating to some of my fellow employees. It's hard to function in the hearing world and when things start going bad, it becomes more difficult to relate. For example, in meetings, the more people in attendance, the harder it is to follow them. "Brainstorming" sessions are particularly difficult where many people are talking at once "bouncing ideas and me off the wall."

I was backed into a corner; and, in desperation, I started using my deafness as a defense. Thankfully, the level heads of my friends prevailed; they jumped all over me. I'd never even come close to doing something like that before; and upon reflection, I realized that they were right and I stopped feeling put-upon and sorry for myself. I continued to work hard and was eventually rewarded with a promotion.

I got transferred to a new group where I was asked to be the CAD manager with the promise of getting into design work. By doing this, I moved out of a situation that I had some trouble handling to one where I proved to myself and to the company that I was good at my job. In the end, I decided not to stick with my position as CAD manager, although I was grateful for everything I learned during my six years in the design groups. But in the end, I decided to return to my original group, Facilities Management, where I felt that there would now be the proper managerial support to allow me to reach my potential.

I learned a lot from those tough experiences. One invaluable lesson is if you have a problem or need something changed, it's best to go through the proper channels." Write a memo or report something formally. This is what I did back in 1995 with electronic mail: I recommended that the office should have electronic mail to help people communicate faster and more efficiently, and do their jobs better. I closed by saying I had a hearing impairment and that e-mail would be a tremendous way for me, in particular, to communicate. Guess what? We got the system and it helped everyone improve their performance.

So, here I am after 16 years with the same firm: I have my own group of 15 that I co-manage, and the work is both challenging and interesting. I have that rare situation in which I am allowed to execute ideas without much restriction. I have good friends and great clients, and I work hard and produce good results.

You might say I'm coming back from the bad old days of 1992 and 1993 when I was derailed from my career goals by becoming a CAD operator instead of an engineer. In hindsight, what I've learned to do is condition my job to fit my disability, which means learning not to get into situations I can't handle. I guess I really am growing up! The lesson in it all? On the job, you need mentors and friends; in short, you need a network. I'm not a great writer, but there are people at work who can take my writing and make it better. To make it work well, it should be a team effort.

But the story wouldn't be complete without a few words about the information age and new technology. For me, the information age came along at just the right time. There are many examples.

Word processors are a tremendous asset. Even today, I struggle with the spelling of words and their proper pronunciation. But thanks to my laptop computer, word processor and grammar checker, I'm constantly checking my spelling and grammar as I write. I probably use the "backspace key" more often than most people. If someone were to read something that I wrote with a pen, they would be more than surprised at how bad my spelling can get.

Similarly, e-mail has been great. It's made it possible for people who are deaf or hard of hearing to remove many communication barriers with coworkers and clients. E-mail makes it easy to get your point across without a lot of chit-chat. Even better, you don't have to worry about missing any words or critical information; it's all right there in black and white (and sometimes color, if you attach a graphic).

The personal pager has also helped. My first pager displayed only a numeric message, which was fine for a while, but frustrating when people left voice messages on my mailbox. That was tough for me to hear, especially when there was very specific information such as phone numbers or statistics. So, I decided to upgrade to one that would display text messages. And just to be sure, I now ask that people leave a text message with an operator who then relays that message to my pager without me ever having to listen to it. I also have e-mail sent directly to my pager and my two-way pager allows me to respond back.

Then there are ways to use a combination of technologies to solve a problem. For example, I moved into a new office as a result of a promotion and was having difficulty with the phone. There were electrical feeders in the wall next to my office that was interfering with the telephone (T-switch) on my hearing aid, making it extremely difficult for me to hear.

By this time I was established in my line of work and needed to use the phone constantly. I thought of the conference room at the League for the Hard of Hearing, which was equipped with a loop system to allow anyone with a hearing aid to listen to the speaker without any extra equipment. A loop system consists of a wire running around a room that acts like a giant speaker coil, without the speaker. Instead of piping sound, it creates an EMF [electromagnetic field] field in the room, so if someone is wearing a hearing aid with a T-switch, the EMF simulates the coil inside the hearing aid and transmits sound to the wearer. It is a wonderful system because it removes all background noise including the electrical feeders in the wall.

I called the director of technical services at the League for the Hard of Hearing and asked him if it were possible for that system to be hooked directly into my telephone. He said he didn't know if that had been tried before, but, if we could connect some devices together, we should be able to get it to work.

I responded promptly, ordered all the required equipment and installed it as soon as possible. We were ready to try it, and what do you know? The system worked even better then I expected. Because I wear body aids, I would normally have to hold the phone upside down against my chest in order to hear. That's cumbersome, because it requires that I bend my neck down in order to speak into the phone. Now, because I pick up the sound from a loop of wire running around my office (not the speaker on the telephone), I can hold the phone like a hearing person: or even put it on the desk when just hearing and make notes with my hands. Today, my clients and colleagues tell me that I also sound better because my mouth is directly on the microphone instead of five inches away.

My final communication hurdle was the cellular phone. Although I had tried a couple of ideas, such as attaching an amplifier to a microphone and speaker attachment used by hearing people, they didn't work. Never one to try to do something by myself, I announced at a team meeting that I would buy dinner for two for the first person who found a device that would allow me to use a cellular phone. Sure enough, through the power of the Internet, one of my coworkers found such a device. I made a simple modification to a device designed for the behind-the-ear hearing aid to be used with my body aids. One of the great things about the information/

technology age is that you are limited only by your imagination. If you have an idea, more likely then not, someone will be able to make it happen for you.

I spoke to a group recently in which I was introduced as "a miracle." I am not a miracle; a miracle means you sit around and something just happens. I was brought up in a hearing environment and worked hard. I willed myself to adjust to and adapt to a hearing environment. It's amazing how many successful people say "I just worked harder then the others." Michael Jordan, Derek Jeter and Tiger Woods have all credited their success to hard work. It's not that they're necessarily smarter then others, or that they were lucky.

That is particularly important to understand, because the last thing I want to do is mislead parents of hearing-impaired children into thinking that their children should follow the very same route that I did. You should learn all that you can about a hearing impairment, and inspire your children to be the best they can be. You should never, ever, compare your hearing-impaired youngster to anyone else. Each child is an individual with their own personality, drive and abilities. What is important is that parents should know how to nurture their child's abilities taking into consideration their strong points and, equally important, their weak points.

Recently, I gave a piece of advice to a friend who is deaf and is currently studying to be a doctor. The advice was "to know your strengths, know your weaknesses and build on both." The point was that there will be some things that she should concede to not being able to do, such as understanding other doctors when their mouths are covered in an operating room. Once acknowledgment is made that verbal communications will not be possible, other means like hand signals can be substituted.

In my own case, I knew that in order to be successful I would have to choose a career that would combine my desire to build things and allow me to live comfortably. If it were not for the desire to live comfortably, I would probably have settled for life as a carpenter or automotive mechanic; but I knew that I had to aim for more. So I thought to myself: How can I make money and also feed my desire to build things? That is how I came upon engineering as a career choice. Once I decided on engineering, there was no stopping me.

A former coworker was really good at his job. He is a great worker between the hours of 9 A.M. and 5 P.M. But the hours at Syska & Hennessy are 8 A.M. to 5 P.M. He always says to me, "I don't know how you guys do it.... You just seem to have more energy then most of us." By "you guys," he means handicapped people. He's right, in a way: If you're handicapped, you just have to have more energy and a willingness to work harder than others. He is just at a different comfort level than I am.

∽

At the risk of being politically incorrect, I feel that parents who work more than they absolutely have to should evaluate how the lost time together is affecting their hearing-impaired child's ability to learn and grow. I fully understand that some mothers have to work just to make ends meet; however, I can say with a great deal of emotion and passion that if my mother hadn't been a homemaker and wasn't available when I arrived home from school to ensure that I did my homework, I wouldn't be enjoying the success I have today.

There were many times that my mother spent the afternoon writing out the words for films and tapes that I was required to listen to in class so that I could read them later on when I had to do my homework. Many times I would get frustrated with the difficulty in comprehending or understanding some topics, and she'd put up with my tantrums and drive the information into my head. And many times, I'd wake up in the morning not wanting to go to school and my mother would find a way to get me out the door and on my way. If I had to point to the most important moments that ensured and defined my success, it would be the afternoons with my mother, doing something I absolutely hated doing, especially when all of my friends were outside playing.

So, I would recommend to teachers and parents that they tell their students and their children that they "can" and not that they "can't." I can't emphasize enough the importance of this positive attitude. A further recommendation for parents, who know their children better they anyone else, is to question authority when a suggestion is made that they feel is not appropriate for their child. P.L. 94-142, or The Education for All Handicapped Children Act, has given parents the right to be involved in planning their children's special education programs. Parents should take advantage of this right and be active participants in planning conferences and become knowledgeable about the needs of their children.

There are still a lot of misconceptions about being deaf. One is that many people feel the handicapped need to be helped all the time. It is really the other way around; instead, it's the handicapped person who should help others feel at ease. Some people don't know how to handle someone with a handicap, so when I'm approached and asked about my hearing aid, I try to be open about it. By doing that, everything is in the open and there are no misunderstandings. Still, there are always people who, no matter how much explaining you try to do, will never understand your handicap. Don't waste time, just move along.

Succeeding at work and overcoming a lot of odds convinces me that I want to give back something to those who can learn from what I have experienced. I want to share some of the lessons I've learned along the way with hearing-impaired people and their parents. Having note takers and sign language interpreters is great for hearing-impaired students. But what happens socially? And what about the work environment, where there are no note takers and things can get tough? Those are areas where I can offer help.

A friend of mine asked me not long ago if I might not have gone as far as I have if I hadn't been deaf. That's hard to say. But there isn't a doubt that I wouldn't be the person I am today if I had not been deaf. In my case, the drive had to come from somewhere inside me. No question that I do not like to lose. When I was a kid and not always the best baseball player, I made a point to find something else that I was good at, such as carpentry, automotive mechanics, and so on. You just build on your strengths.

A few years ago, President Bush (the elder) described volunteerism as "1,000 points of light." His point was that one of the best ways to ensure that the needs of society are met is for individuals to give back based on a skill or quality they possess. It was through his analogy and because of the support that I have received that I realized I had something to give back. I had to find a point of light that could make me shine.

My proudest accomplishment, which turned out to be the point of light I had been looking for, is something that I still do today: By speaking well and sharing my experiences with parents of hearing-impaired children, I can help lessen their anxieties. I level with the parents by telling them that in order for their hearing-impaired child to be successful, it will require hard work by everyone — the teachers, the siblings, the relatives and, of course, the parents.

What I don't like hearing are parents who tell me that I'm great. I tell them that their hearing-impaired son or daughter can do it as well. The primary responsibility has to come from their child. The guidance and encouragement is nice, but it has to be focused on the child helping him/herself. But if serving as a role model for handicapped children and adults can benefit someone, then I am proud to do so.

As well as speaking to parents of hearing-impaired children, I am also involved in the League for the Hard of Hearing's mentor program. This program is a golden opportunity for hearing-impaired students in a mainstream high school environment to talk and meet successful hearing-impaired adults.

When I was introduced at the League for the Hard of Hearing's awards luncheon where I received my Personal Achievement Award, I was cited for "serving as an example for numerous deaf and hard of hearing young people" and for "offering practical advice and the unvarnished truth on coping with a disability in the hearing world." When the words "unvarnished truth" were spoken, it was then that I realized the importance of speaking well and sharing my experiences — both good and bad — with people going through what I have already done. In my speech, I thanked numerous individuals for their contribution to my success, from my sister, who had to suffer from less attention, to my doctor who always enlightened me, to my family and friends who supported me, to my clients and coworkers who helped make me successful and obviously to my parents for giving me their unselfish best.

One of my college professors told me that one of the things he liked about me was that I didn't worry about what anyone does or thinks. The same applies at work, where I don't let anyone stop me from moving forward. The only possession that nobody can take from you is your knowledge. So it goes that there are times that in order to gain knowledge, you must endure some pain. That is one of my favorite sayings. There is a lot of truth to that.

Look at my parents, who, in hindsight, were the real motivational team. My mother had the hardest job, making sure I did my homework. Then there was my dad, who made sure I had fun by creating the airplane club, in which all the kids in the neighborhood joined. The house that I grew up in is the one where I live today and is filled with love, pride and admiration.

Socializing is easier for me these days. I have become involved in my community by working with my church, the Knights of Columbus and the League for the Hard of Hearing. I also enjoy playing golf, which is often a social event because I do it related to community or work functions. If a carnival event requires that I do something physical such as cooking, running a gambling booth or simply cleaning up, I tend to enjoy it more then if I were just a visitor to the event. I find that a combination of doing something physical within a social event is the most enjoyable and satisfying way for me to socialize.

Find me a successful person who said they did it by themselves and I'll tell you that they are mistaken. That goes particularly for successful deaf people. There is no possible way someone in my situation could do what I did without the unconditional support and love from the people around them. For me, that support runs the gamut, from the next-door neighbors (Frank Delibro) who befriended me when the neighborhood kids were picking on me to my parents and grandparents who were there for me, and to my coworkers and friends, who do the extra little things to make my job easier.

Let me return to the start of this story to the little blue engine that said to me "ack a dunde, ack a dunde." My hearing aids correctly told me "I think I can, I think I can." My subsequent struggles and hard work have now given me a new rendition of the train story which I pass on to all hearing impaired children as their theme song: "I knew I could, I knew I could, I knew I could, and I DID!"

That, along with the support of people like Paul Falvey, Dr. Robert Solomon, my physician of infinite wisdom, and Beatrice Spear, my teacher, helped me along the way. So did my wife, Lisa, who entered the story late, but put on the final touches, which assured my success. Their patience speaks loudly of the importance of a team effort and how people should never tackle life's challenges by themselves.

Kathleen Suffridge Treni

RAMSEY, NEW JERSEY

A native of Cincinnati, Kathleen Suffridge Treni has an undergraduate and a graduate degree from the University of Miami, Coral Gables, Florida. After years of teaching deaf and hard of hearing children, she earned a master's in educational psychology and practiced as a psychologist for a brief period. Today, she is an administrator of the Bergen County, New Jersey, Special Services, where she directs the deaf and hard-of-hearing programs. She is an accomplished pianist and the mother of three daughters.

⊷

One of the most frequent issues you hear from people with disabilities who have excelled and overcome barriers is the ability to compensate for their disability. Again and again, one hears about those who beat the odds because of some internal driving force or motivation to rise to the occasion. Most of us have had our share of comments like "you can't do this" or "we couldn't do that." It is unfortunate that many believe these naysayers and conform to the expectations that others set for them.

But for many, the motivation to overcome or to "compensate" is so strong that for these individuals, it becomes a lifelong challenge to demonstrate that anything is possible with faith, hard work and a positive outlook in life.

There are many successful oral deaf adults who have learned to compensate for their lack of hearing. The desire to excel is why some of us succeed in spite of the disability. That is why those of us who are deaf or hard of hearing will do whatever it takes to achieve our goals in order to succeed

133

in the world. For a child with hearing loss, the secret is to turn that hearing impairment into an advantage and to develop ways to compensate for it by challenging the child in creative, different ways.

My brother Mark and I were both born deaf in Cincinnati during the early 1950s. As I was the first-born, it wasn't until I was 15 months old that my parents learned about my hearing loss. Apparently, I had stuck something into my nose and while an ear, nose and throat doctor took care

Kathleen Suffridge Treni

of that problem, he noticed I didn't respond to any noises. After a few tries with an old-fashioned tuning fork, he gently broke the news to my mother. "Oh, no, she isn't deaf," Mom told him. "Kathi is very bright and lets me know in her own way what she wants." But, the doctor showed my mother how I didn't respond to any of the tests and told her that I would never be able to talk.

That was just about the time, in the early '50s, that transistor hearing aids were coming out, making them among the first wave of hearing aids. I got one, a big body aid, with buttons in my ears. My mother wanted to get back to the doctor and say, "I'll show you that my daughter will talk." By then, my mother had made some contacts with different sources. There were far fewer options for deaf children than there are available today. In Cincinnati in those days, you either kept your child in an oral program in your home school district, or you sent your child away to a school for the deaf that used manual communication. At that time, attending a school for the deaf meant a child would sign and get no speech at all.

Back then, your options were one or the other. The term "total communication" had not yet been created. Given only two options from which to choose, my mother's choice was clear: She was going to do everything she could to keep us at home, so we could be a part of the family and be as independent as possible. So, Mark and I went to our local public schools. Mark attended self-contained classes taught by a teacher for the oral deaf, while I attended regular classes with daily pull-out sessions with a speech and language therapist.

What was the source of my mother's drive? I think it was her intellectual curiosity, combined with the importance of having her children home with her. My mother was determined that she wasn't going to take "no" for an answer. Her background in education helped tremendously, but her primary motivation was to help her children grow up to be independent and functioning adults.

As a young child, I received speech therapy — lip-reading and speech articulation — at a speech and hearing clinic. I was brought up with an emphasis on speech reading, and not so much on the auditory listening methods used often today. Therapy was often kinesthetic, with hand positions over my throat and nose to feel the differences in sound productions. Blowing tissues and candles were commonplace to watch and monitor airflow. Today's more auditory emphasis is much better and more refined; many of today's children are using their listening skills better than my generation. Technology has made that possible. My first instincts are to watch a person's face and read lips, because that is my first way to communicate. Today, many children with hearing loss do not always have to do that.

I don't remember much about my preschool deaf classes. I just remember being there — the two-way mirrors that the mothers sat behind to watch the classes and learn techniques they could apply at home. I remember my mother working with Mark and me, using big cards with pictures. I had to take them around the house, matching the picture cards to the pieces of furniture or appliances. I still remember those at-home lessons, which were like a game and could be a lot of fun. Mother got lots of good ideas from the John Tracy Clinic correspondence program. I also remember the long bus rides and the transfers from one bus to another to get to class. No one had second cars in those days; going to the Cincinnati Speech and Hearing Center was a full-day affair.

By the time I got to kindergarten, I was reasonably verbal. A decision had to be made about my educational placement. In a sense, I was somewhere in ability between a self-contained and a regular class, meaning there really wasn't an appropriate class for me. So, I was put into a challenging regular kindergarten, and actually, I attended two kindergarten sessions to boost my language and readiness skills. That set the pattern, although it wasn't easy. I was mainstreamed throughout school although the term "mainstreaming" was unheard of in the 1950s and '60s. I was able to get a regular education, interspersed with speech every day.

❖

If a child is discovered to have a hearing loss during toddler years, then it is expected that language will be delayed. Parents of hearing impaired children need to learn and accept that. It's important that deaf and hard of hearing children learn how to compensate for their language delays with the right educational coaching. It is also imperative that children be taught how to deal with those who have no tolerance for them.

From a young age it is critical that deaf and hard of hearing children know and understand that there will always be kids who will poke fun at them or ignore them. But, if parents teach and guide them with love and with a sense of humor, they'll learn to accept that it's perfectly okay not being friends with everybody. They'll also learn that not everyone is going to take the time to understand them, but that there will be others who will. That is something I tell the parents of children with hearing loss.

Technological advances have been phenomenal, but parents shouldn't expect their hearing impaired children to follow perfectly in all listening environments. They should understand that their child's adjustment to the world is a two-way street; teaching a child to manipulate the environment to make it easier to understand is an important skill. By adjusting lighting, cutting out background noise, using FMs or sound field systems, or asking people to speak a little more clearly are all strategies to make the listening environment easier. For parents, raising a deaf child takes a real willingness to make accommodations.

That goes for friends, as well. My mother always told me you don't need a lot of friends to prove you're somebody; just have a couple of good friends and you'll be okay. I took her advice and had a few good childhood friends who helped get me all the way through school, socially. They were always there for me — and I was there for them, too!

I had the advantage of growing up in the same house on a dead-end street where there were always kids to play with. In those days, social activities were usually confined to the neighborhood, which meant there were always kids around to play pick-up games, like kick-the-can and blindman's buff, with baseball as the all-time favorite in the field at the end of the street. Social activities were initiated by us children in the street; they were spontaneous and relaxed.

Today, however, most kids attend organized activities like dance or karate classes — and except for very rare circumstances, children don't really develop socialization in the neighborhood setting much anymore. The challenge for parents then is to help direct their deaf or hard of hearing child to find their friends at these classes or sports practices. Today, that's the way it works.

∽

My parents always stressed academics over socialization. This doesn't mean all parents of deaf children must do the same: My parents were teachers, so they were naturally interested in having Mark and me excel in our studies. In high school, it was hard socially: I wasn't interested in going to football games, even though my mother tried to encourage me to go. I preferred to be home practicing the piano. To some people, that seems absurd. But, different people have different tastes; mine was music.

I joined a lot of clubs in high school because I functioned better socially in organized activities. It was hard to socialize informally because I couldn't talk on the telephone — there was no TTY in those days and I had no way to communicate with my friends once I was home, unless my mother made the calls. I see my teenage daughters now and how they live on the phone! I missed that period of my life, and didn't connect hourly with girlfriends in the evening hours.

Looking back, I had some real low periods, the first of which came between fifth and sixth grades when I hit a real academic slump. Up until then, I excelled in my studies, but in fifth grade, the subjects became so vocabulary-loaded, and the language of science, social studies, and English became overwhelming such that I couldn't keep up with the language demands. There was too much to assimilate in too little time, and because I wasn't feeling too good about that, I let it affect me socially as well.

Keep in mind that's about the time girls start forming cliques. I see it today with my own daughters. There is a lot of pairing off into small groups and whispering. I just wasn't part of the gossip circles. Sometimes, I preferred to play with someone several years younger than myself! So, I just spent more time on piano and schoolwork at which time my parents sent me to a small, private girls' school. That was for seventh grade, when I slowly started to rebuild my self-esteem. The classes were small and there was a lot of individual attention given to all the girls.

Music was an immense help for both my speech and self-esteem. I was seven when I became interested in piano. By listening very carefully to the keys of the piano — I could only hear the lower octaves — I could discriminate and try to match my voice to the vibrations. It was also around then that I got a songbook with pictures that I used to learn the words to songs. Today I use that same book to teach the songs to my two younger daughters, Ashley and Morgan.

I had another big advantage — my grandmother, whom I adoringly called "Gran-Gran," who believed in me from the start. Gran-Gran was a Knoxville, Tennessee, dress shop saleswoman who recognized when I was 11 that music was a long-term interest for me, and saved up every penny she could to buy me a new piano. Gran-Gran was the kind of woman who just knew I was going to make it: "You're going to be just fine," she would say to me. Her faith rubbed off on me. She had nearly nothing, but she was very rich. She was my inspiration, and just didn't let my hearing loss get in the way of anything I could or couldn't do.

Our family didn't have the financial resources for me to continue at private school, but I did have three good years there. Back I went to the public high school for my final three years, and I sailed through academically. It was very easy, because I had developed the discipline and the strategies to do well. It became a cycle: I did well in school, which helped my self-confidence and, in turn, helped me socially.

I think the circumstances under which I grew up forced me, in a sense, to become the way I am today — an individualist. At the University of Miami, I had several opportunities to join sororities, but I chose not to because I just wasn't interested. Instead, I was more involved in Tri Beta, the honorary biology club, which I served as an officer, and enjoyed trips to study ecosystems of the Dry Tortugas, the Everglades and the cypress swamps. By then, I feel that I had matured and was selective about activities that interested me. My interests were so diversified in college that I was inducted into the Mortar Board honor society for women and became its president during my senior year.

When I talk to parents about socialization and maturation, I ask that they be patient with their deaf and hard of hearing children because, for the most part, social skills do mature later than their hearing peers. After all, hearing children learn rules through incidental listening. Developmentally, deaf and hard of hearing children are several years behind, and that's okay, as long as you are helping your child along with the process. It is not uncommon for deaf or hard of hearing children to repeat a grade just to give them a chance to mature socially and become more responsible for their learning.

Another area that is commonplace among deaf and hard of hearing children is their self-centeredness. It is a problem people may have to work with gently in order to help the child along. The nature of the disability forces parents to work and communicate directly to the child at all times. In turn, the child has gotten used to the extra attention and begins to lack development of feelings and thoughtfulness for others. Role-playing and conversation in scenarios helps deaf and hard of hearing children think about their actions and choice of words.

Most families face some kind of challenge. We were no exception, and among my problems was having a loving, but very unstable, father. My mother was the strong one who gave Mark and me the structure to build our lives. Because my father suffered from a mental illness that prevented him from being fully-functioning, my mother was the one who had to perform a lot of family management. In turn, her strength, and the way she dealt with problems, became my strength. While my parents stayed together for most of my childhood, they finally got divorced just about the time I graduated from high school. I share this part because stories about successful oral deaf adults do not only come from places where people have money or resources or "connections." I lived in a very complicated household, and it was not easy to rise above the difficulties we had at home.

I graduated from the University of Miami with the double degree, and then received a master's degree in deaf education. In college, as much as I loved the study of biology and doing ecosystem research in Florida habitats, I came to realize that I am very much a "people person" and preferred to teach. In doing so, I joined the noble profession of five generations of educators and ministers in my mother's family. And, in teaching deaf kids, I knew I would have an advantage: an automatic understanding of their challenges.

I started working with the deaf in 1975, when my husband Michael accepted a position as a professor at Berklee College of Music in Boston. Because there wasn't a school in Boston that would hire a deaf teacher to teach oral children, I accepted the job at the Jackson Mann School, which that very year had become a total communication program. I quickly took an evening sign language class at Boston University so I could perform my duties there. I wasn't happy with this new philosophy where teachers stopped using FM systems and discouraged children to use their voices while they signed.

There is a time and place for everything. It so happened in the summer of 1976 at the A.G. Bell Convention in Boston, where I met the director of a very successful oral program in Bergen County, New Jersey. We talked and she offered me a job — not seeing my deafness as a deterrent in my ability to teach. I jumped at the opportunity, and I'm still there today!

Michael and I met in the University of Miami Music School. I was there after getting special permission to take private piano lessons in lieu of "Introduction to Music 101," which involved a lot of listening to records, which I wouldn't have been able to handle with my 110-decibel hearing loss. At the end of my junior year, I gave a recital even though it was required only of music majors. It was while practicing for the concert that I met Michael, who was practicing for his senior recital. We frequently talked between practices, and I invited him to play in my piano recital. Michael is still involved in music. Although he has been involved in other business ventures, his latest is a musical play about the life of Alexander Graham Bell.

Just recently, Michael found an old recording of my college recital. I remember that concert well: It was in 1973 and the recital hall was filled. I heard it for the first time in over 20 years. With my cochlear implant, I could hear it! I asked Michael to find my book and I followed along as if it were yesterday. Listening to that concert was a very emotional experience for me.

ᕕᕗ

Michael and I have three daughters, Tiffany, Ashley and Morgan. Sure, there are challenges in being the deaf parent of hearing children, and there always will be. My house was wired from top to bottom when they were babies: I had baby criers, and lights that blinked off and on when the doorbell or phone or fire alarm went off. My first baby slept on a mattress on the floor, so she could crawl over to my bed to get my attention when she needed me. Our daughters all learned to look at me straight in the face, or they knew they would get no response from me. Today, I truly believe their clear enunciation and lovely singing voices were developed because they had developed, in part, a system to communicate to me clearly.

In the community, I found it difficult meeting the parents of my daughters' friends as I did participating in PTA. At home, I noticed that the dinner hour was becoming increasingly difficult as they chatted away about their experiences in school. I began to realize that I was going to miss a great deal of my children's lives — their piano recitals and their speeches. I hated having to applaud them for a job well done when I couldn't hear them speak or perform music. I felt like a hypocrite.

❧

Wanting to share more in the lives of my children was one of many reasons I got a cochlear implant in 1992. I felt if I could make life easier for our family on many levels, it would be worth the surgery — and I just didn't want my daughters to have to accommodate me.

The implant has made a wonderful difference. I never dreamed that years later, I would be attending dozens of musicals and concerts to hear all three of my daughters sing in principal roles and as soloists in choruses. I have heard my husband's creative and brilliant Broadway caliber production of BELL, and I can now use the telephone for the first time in my life. Even the dinner conversations are more manageable.

As a director in the Bergen County Special Services, I have a big responsibility of managing a talented and dedicated staff of professionals committed to educating deaf and hard-of-hearing children. Technology has improved so much over the last 10 years alone that the field of deaf education is evolving into new levels of service delivery models. I am amazed by what children are able to do now at a much younger age than was ever possible 25 years ago when I entered the profession.

After all, we oral deaf adults, most of whom you are reading about in this very book, are from a different generation that is no longer relevant in today's educational milieu. We're now of the "old school" — those who thrived on so little residual hearing that we made it through lipreading, primarily.

My friend, Mildred Oberkotter, says we are the generation of visual oral deaf— we who fixate our eyes on people's faces to pick up every clue, every eyebrow movement and every emotion to help us comprehend what is being communicated. It was our generation with whom speech therapists made the most of tactile clues to help us learn to talk, where we learned by how it felt to say sounds correctly. It was an age when we wore huge, heavy body aids with "Frankenstein" buttons and hard plastic ear molds that never seemed to fit properly.

We are the generation that never had services to help us function easier in our classes in high school or college; note takers and interpreters were unheard of back then. We are the generation that learned that we had to give at least 50 percent more effort to gain the benefits and rewards of our efforts. In the 1970s and '80s, we were the generation who had no difficulty using an oral interpreter to help us with lectures because we lip-read perfectly, without the need for sound. And strangest of all, there was a time when parents of deaf or hard of hearing children would be thrilled and would cry to hear an oral deaf adult speak at all, never minding the nasal qualities and articulation errors that came with the spoken word.

There is a kindred spirit among those of us who share this background. Yes, a chapter of visual oral deaf adults is closing as the more auditory dependent deaf and hard of hearing leaders take center stage. I salute the new generation with pride!

Bonnie Poitras Tucker

TEMPE, ARIZONA

Bonnie Poitras Tucker is an attorney and a professor of law at Arizona State University. An authority on disability law, she has written eight books and more than 100 articles, including The Feel of Silence *(Temple University Press, 1995), an acclaimed first-person account of life as an oral deaf person, and* Cochlear Implants: A Handbook *(McFarland & Company, 1998). The Feel of Silence has proven so successful in Germany that it is now being published in paperback there and the German* Reader's Digest *will issue a condensed version of the book.*

Professor Tucker has received outstanding alumni awards from both Syracuse University and the University of Colorado School of Law and was awarded the Phoenix Mayor's Award. She is a frequent lecturer at conferences and conventions.

My book, *The Feel of Silence*, was originally going to be a collection of excerpts — the ones that appear in the book, plus many others. It was not going to be an autobiography. Have you read the book, *Everything I Learned, I Learned in Kindergarten?* It was going to be that kind of a book.

But all the publishers said I needed to write an autobiography. I didn't want to write one; that was never my intention. But finally — to get the message across — I agreed to do it. The message is directed to "the man in the street" to explain what deafness is all about, because basically, people don't have a clue. Even people who work professionally with deaf people, in my opinion, don't understand a lot about deafness.

One of the things that really spurred me on to write the book was a conversation I had with another deaf author. We were talking about education, and how difficult it was when we were growing up for deaf children in the mainstream setting of public schools. In my case, it was difficult to make friends in school; I couldn't understand much of what was going on, and life was really pretty crummy at the time. My author friend said he'd gone through all those things as well. But he didn't talk about that in his autobiographical book. So, I felt the book didn't present a fair picture of what deafness

Bonnie Tucker

really means. I wanted a book out there that really explains about what it means to be deaf.

Reaction to the book has been very, very positive. Much of the reaction has come from hearing people who have written or called to say that they had no idea what deafness really meant, and that they learned about a whole new aspect of life they'd never thought about before. Some of the letters and calls have come from fellow law professors who've said things such as, "What an eye opener!" Others have been from people who like to read books — just hearing people who know nothing about deafness and many deaf people have written or called to say how much they could relate to the book, and to thank me for writing it.

I received my cochlear implant in 1991 at the age of 52. Life is easier with the implant; no question about it. At the same time, the implant presents other frustrations. For example, before my implant, I might be in an airplane and there'd be an announcement; back then, I didn't know when there was an announcement. Today, however, I know there's someone speaking, but I have no idea whether the pilot is saying something important, or talking about the weather, or telling a joke. I ask the flight attendants innumerable times what's being said, but I can't count on their help. So now, in some respects, it's even more frustrating because I'm aware of what I'm missing. Sometimes, oblivion is a good thing!

At times, deaf people with implants have to deal with unreasonable expectations. Not many people know I have an implant. And the people who do know about my implant realize that while it helps quite a bit, I am still deaf. But I do know people who said to others with implants, "you have a cochlear implant, so you can hear." That's not true, so you have to educate people.

Today, there may be more awareness — but not acceptance — of people with disabilities. People are just not sensitive. To that end, my advice to the parent of a child who is deaf or hard of hearing is to get the child an implant as soon as possible. Get the child an implant as early as 18 months, if possible, and treat that child as if he or she is hearing. Then, put that child in a good auditory/verbal program and "go for it." Add to that, the parental commitment; the parents have to be ready to give the time and commitment to their child.

Adolescence is a difficult time for most people. It's doubly difficult when you have a disability. For me, the hardest time may have been when I was getting a divorce — that and my teenage years were probably the hardest for me.

As a deaf person, you have to work harder than your hearing peers. I was driving recently to a television appearance in Massachusetts and traveling with a hearing woman who said she got 90 percent of her news information from the radio. Everyone I know turns the radio on when they're driving to and from work. By the time they get to work in the morning, they know a lot of news that I don't know. We deaf people miss a tremendous amount of information.

Growing up, I never heard radio nor heard a television show. So, I missed an enormous amount. If you talk to me about things that happened on television in those days, generally I don't know about them; I missed all of that. On the other hand, people tell me that by not listening to, say, call-in shows on the radio, I'm not missing anything. It's true, but it's not true at the same time because by listening to something like that, you're picking up little pieces of information, whether you think that information is worthwhile or not.

So, it's just unreasonable to say that I don't miss much. What I miss is the choice of whether to listen or not. And I miss all those little things that are trivial; I know they're trivial and I know they're tidbits, but together, they make up a big picture. Deaf people miss all those trivial things and that sometimes make it difficult for them to mix socially with other people.

That's a subtle point. People sit around and make small talk, and deaf people, when they're talking with hearing people, are not always able to engage to the same extent.

So, how do I pick up the things I miss on the radio driving to work? I have to read the newspaper, which takes time. To get that kind of information, I have to find at least 20 minutes to read the newspaper — and I'm a fast reader.

That gets back to an earlier point: As a deaf person, you just have to develop the ability to concentrate. I get up at 5:00 A.M. every morning to read the paper, so I know what's happening. Basically, I have to be very alert and that's true particularly after I get to work. Deaf people can't sit back and relax because all the time, even if I am not looking directly at a person, I'm always watching for people out of the corner of my eye. It's more work to mix in and get basic information.

At the same time, a large part of succeeding is just personality. Let's face it, among the hearing population, a lot of people are perfectly satisfied having blue-collar jobs and are not interested in having a job where they have to work 60 hours or 80 hours a week. That's okay; it's a matter of personality. I think you're going to find the same differences among deaf people as you find among hearing people. But at the same time, there are those who would say that because I'm deaf, I've got to do more to show society that a deaf person can "cut it." I know that's true, and I'm willing to do it.

I do a lot of public speaking, which is my way of giving back. In addition to *The Feel of Silence*, which was a personal book, I write other books that are meant to help parents of deaf children and other deaf people. My motive in writing these books is purely altruistic, For example, I get so many calls from parents wanting to know "What am I going to do with the school district that won't help my child?" There are parents out there who are desperate; there's just nobody to help them. That's why I wrote my question and answer book.

I have also written extensively about cochlear implants. That is another way of giving back. I get so frustrated because there are so many parents who don't know that this wonderful technology is there for their child. Or, they've been bamboozled by the Deaf Culturists into thinking that by taking advantage of an implant, they'll be making their child into something he or she is not.

I wanted to do the cochlear implant book because I want to refute the comments by Deaf Culturists who keep saying there's no evidence out there that cochlear implants help children to develop language. That's just malarkey; all you have to do is to look at the progress these kids are making and you can refute these statements.

One of the ways that deaf oralists can really help in defeating the arguments of the Deaf Culturists is simply to band together. We are not organized as we should be. What we need to do is to get all the oral deaf organizations together — Cochlear Implant Club International, Auditory Verbal International and SHHH [Self Help for the Hard of Hearing People] among them. Under the guidance of A.G. Bell, we need to form a coalition to create a very strong public relations campaign. We don't have that at the moment and I think that's unfortunate. We really need it.

There's no question that the Deaf Culturists are winning the public relations battle. In at least 10 states, they've already won the educational battle. Deaf children in those states cannot get an oral education unless they have private money. Arizona, where I live, is one of those states, although the Oberkotter Foundation has started a school for oral deaf children in Phoenix, which, of course, means that parents need funding to send their children there.

Otherwise, their children face a future in which they're immersed in Deaf Culture. If I had a dime for every phone call I've had from parents all over the country facing that dilemma in their own states, I'd be rich. There's no reason for that. We oralists should have won that public relations battle 10 years ago.

Realistically, we have to understand that society is not going to change. We can't expect society to change. People have their own lives and their own agendas and they just don't have the time to make all the everyday accommodations that need to be made for people with disabilities.

Therefore, it's up to us to use technology to chip away at hearing loss. That's why I believe so strongly in the cochlear implant; that's our way of eliminating the problem. You can't sit back and say that society is going to make all the adaptations. I believe that we deaf people have a lot of responsibility. That's where I differ from the Deaf Culturists. They feel that society has to make all the accommodations, whereas I feel that deaf people have to make the majority of adaptations. We have to do what we can to be a part of hearing society because that's the way of the world.

Helpful Resources

Organizations:

- **The Alexander Graham Bell Association for the Deaf and Hard of Hearing** (www.agbell.org) is one of the world's largest organizations and information centers on pediatric hearing loss and the auditory approach. A.G. Bell focuses specifically on children with hearing loss, providing ongoing support and advocacy for parents, professionals and other interested parties. Its quarterly magazine is *Volta Voices* (*see* Magazines). A.G. Bell and its magazine are rich resources of information related to all aspects of hearing loss.

- **The Cochlear Implant Association, Inc.** (www.ciai.org) is a nonprofit organization for cochlear implant recipients, their families, professionals and others interested in cochlear implants. The Association provides support and information to anyone with a cochlear implant or a child with an implant. Their quarterly magazine is *Contact* (*see* Magazines).

- **The Combined Health Information Database** (http://chid.nih.gov) is a reference tool that leads health professionals, patients and others to thousands of journal articles and patient education materials that contain information about different health topics. CHID has 16 subject areas or "subfiles"—each a rich source of hard-to-find literature that is not often referenced in other databases. CHID's Deafness and Communication Disorders subfile contains citations to more than 4,000 publications.

- **The Deafness Research Foundation** (www.drf.org) is a voluntary health organization committed to curing and preventing all forms of hearing loss and making lifelong hearing health a U.S. national priority by funding research and educating government and the public. DRF is, in effect, the "venture capital" arm of hearing research, annually awarding grants to promising young researchers and to established researchers to explore new avenues of hearing science. This seed money has led to dramatic innovations that have contributed to the diagnosis and treatment of otitis media (middle ear infections), the cochlear implant, implantable hearing aids, breakthroughs in molecular biology and the regeneration of inner ear hair cells.

- **The John Tracy Clinic** (www.johntracy.org) was founded by Spencer Tracy's wife, Louise, in 1942 and named for their son John who was diagnosed with profound hearing loss but learned to speak. The Los Angeles–based Tracy Clinic offers free online and mail courses for parents of deaf and hard of hearing babies and preschoolers, as well as parents of young deaf-blind children. Families receive lessons and videotapes offering information on language, auditory learning, speech and child development. Services include a correspondence and distance education program for parents of children up to five years, as well as intensive three-week summer sessions for parents and their children.

- **The League for the Hard of Hearing** (www.lhh.org) is a New York City–based private, not-for-profit rehabilitation agency for infants, children and adults who are hard of hearing and deaf. The League's Mission is to improve the quality of life for people with all degrees of hearing loss, which is accomplished by providing hearing rehabilitation and human service programs for people who are hard of hearing and deaf, and their families, regardless of age or mode of communication. Founded in 1910, the League aims to empower consumers and professionals to provide leadership to disciplines that relate to hearing rehabilitation and promotes hearing conservation and public education about hearing. Included at League headquarters is the first Museum of Hearing in the northeast United States.

- **The Oral Deaf Education Web Site** (www.oraldeaf.org), a product of the Oberkotter Foundation, provides practical advice and information through a range of oral deaf literature, tapes (see Videotapes) and other resources. Available at no cost are the inspiring tapes, Speaking for Myself and Dreams Spoken Here, as well as the parent resource kit, Make a Joyful Noise. The web site also lists information for professionals, undergraduate and graduate schools offering degrees in speech therapy and oral education, and job openings.

- **Self Help for the Hard of Hearing People, Inc.** (www.shhh.org) is a consumer and educational organization devoted to the welfare and interests of hard of hearing people, their relatives and friends. SHHH strives to improve the quality of hard of hearing people's lives through education, advocacy and self-help.

Other Web Sites:

- **The About Network** (www.deafness.aboutcom/health/deafness/library.com)

- **The Cochlear Implant Research Center at the University of Iowa** (www.medicine.uiowa.edu/otolaryngology).

Other Sources:

- A good way to find a specialist is to contact a university hospital's Department of Otolaryngology or refer to The Official ABMS Directory of Board Certified Medical Specialists, published by Marquis Who's Who, and available at most local libraries.

- The kit, **Make a Joyful Noise** (www.oraldeaf.org), provides pediatric professionals and parents with the resources and information they need to make educational and medical choices for deaf or hard-of-hearing children. Available free of charge from the Oberkotter Foundation, it addresses the importance of early intervention to maximize a newly-identified deaf or hard-of-hearing child's ability to listen and speak. Includes a handbook to help parents make informed decisions and a suggested parent reading list.

- **The Clarke School for the Deaf/Center for Oral Education** (www.clarke school.org) is among the most prestigious schools offering oral education for deaf children. The main campus is in Northampton, Massachusetts, and the school has recently opened auditory/oral centers in Jacksonville, Florida and New York City, with another scheduled for Philadelphia. The web site provides a good introduction to oral education for parents.

Books:

- *Cochlear Implants: A Handbook* (McFarland & Company, 1998) by Bonnie Poitras Tucker. Explains, in a simple and accessible style, how implants work, for whom and the extent to which they help deaf people hear. Includes Tucker's own experience with the implant procedure, along with its advantages and benefits, and includes a comprehensive explanation of the basic concept, history and evolution of implants.

- *Communication Access for People with Hearing Loss: Compliance with the Americans with Disabilities Act* (York Press, 1994) edited by Dr. Mark Ross. The Americans with Disabilities Act of 1990 mandates communication access for people with hearing loss. Yet most people have little knowledge of this federal law, particularly the provisions to assist people who are deaf or hard of hearing. What accommodations do businesses, organizations and institutions have to provide under the law? Is ignorance bliss? Or an acceptable excuse? If an event provides an ASL interpreter does that cover the needs? With the guiding idea that technology is a tool and not a solution, 17 professionals discuss access for people who use manual or oral communication methods in terms of the law, current technology and trends.

- *The Feel of Silence* (Temple University Press, 1995) by Bonnie Poitras Tucker. This memoir is the autobiography of an inspiring deaf woman who overcame extraordinary obstacles to become a law professor at Arizona State University.

- *Hear Again: Back to Life with a Cochlear Implant* (League for the Hard of Hearing, 1999) by Arlene Romoff. The compelling biography of how a late-deafened adult regained communication with the "hearing" world with the aid of a cochlear implant. Romoff shared her experiences, via e-mail, with family, friends and colleagues, which comprise the basis of the book.

- *Hear What You've Been Missing: How to Cope with Hearing Loss* (John Wiley & Sons, 1998) by Donna S. Wayner, Ph.D. The Director of the Hearing Center at the Albany, New York, Medical Center addresses the sense of frustration and isolation via a series of common questions and practical answers developed during her years of clinical experience as head of the Hearing Center's diagnostic and rehabilitative audiology services. Along the way, the book outlines many tools and strategies available to overcome the effects of hearing loss and offers solutions to communicate in social situations, enjoy music, radio and television, improve work or school performance, and to properly evaluate available assistive listening device options.

- *The Hearing-Impaired Child: Infancy Through High School Years* (Andover Medical Publishers, 1992) by Drs. Antonia Brancia Maxon and Diane Brackett. Provides audiologists and speech-language pathologists with essential information to guide the diagnosis and treatment of children who are deaf or hard of hearing. It addresses specific management techniques for three age ranges (infant–toddler, pre-schooler and school-age) and discusses the child's needs in terms of family and economic considerations.

- *Hearing-Impaired Children in the Mainstream* (York Press, 1990) edited by Dr. Mark Ross. Inclusion? Mainstreaming? Or special School for the Deaf? These educational options continue to be hotly debated. Here is a comprehensive and authoritative perspective on integrating the child who is hard of hearing or deaf into the regular classroom. Seventeen experts contribute their experience and practical strategies to this beneficial resource for audiologists, speech language pathologists, classroom teachers and parents. "Appropriate education, and not mainstreaming, is the issue," writes Ross. "It is the children and their needs that must drive the educational process and their interests must be the focus of all our efforts."

- *Hearing Loss* (Franklin Watts, Inc., 1991) by Karin Mango. This straightforward book, complete with illustrations and photographs, explains how the human ear works, what causes hearing loss and strategies to deal with it. Focuses on conservation of hearing, technological innovations, hearing-ear dogs, as well as illuminating the historic debate surrounding the signing versus oral debate.

- *Listening with My Heart* (Doubleday, 1997) by Heather Whitestone. Talk about a role model, from a deaf childhood to Miss Alabama and finally, Miss America 1995.

- *Reading Between the Lips* (Bonus Books, 1995) by Lew Golan. A newspaper editor, turned advertising copywriter, turned computer guru, turned social and political activist, the upbeat Golan tells the story of being a profoundly deaf man in mainstream society.

- *What's That Pig Outdoors? A Memoir of Deafness* (Hill & Wang, 1990) by Henry Kisor. A veteran newspaper reporter, Kisor tells the story of his life in this witty, wise memoir.

- *When the Hearing Gets Hard: Winning the Battle Against Hearing Impairment* (Persons Books, 1993) by Elaine Suss. The writer herself has a severe hearing loss, and brings sensitivity, compassion, and humor along with survival strategies to the issues of a range of issues from family and workplace challenges to strategies for travel, shopping, eating out and going to the movies … Includes helpful insight on medications that may cause deafness, harmful noise pollution and assistive devices.

- *Yes, You Can Heather: The Story of Heather Whitestone, Miss America 1995* (HarperCollins, 1995) by Daphne Gray. Heather Whitestone's improbable journey, courtesy of her mom.

Magazines

- *Contact* is quarterly for members and friends of the Cochlear Implant Club Association, Inc. (CICA) is another good resource of information for families involved in oral deaf education. Articles from a recent issue: "An All-Implant Family," "Assistive Hearing Devices in the Business Context," "Software for Children with Cochlear Implants" and "Music and the Cochlear Implant: Realistic Expectations."

- *Hearing Heath* is designed for people who experience any degree of hearing loss, tinnitus, or other ear disorders. From the dangers of loud noise to training hearing dogs to the controversy surrounding sign language vs. oral communication and cochlear implants, the magazine, published every two months, covers a range of topics important for living with hearing impairment and deafness.

- *The Volta Review* is a highly respected research journal that brings the latest theories, research, current perspectives, and practical guidance from noted specialists in education, audiology, speech and language science and psychology.

- *Volta Voices* is A.G. Bell's bimonthly magazine containing articles about all aspects of deafness from education to technology and advocacy. It is sent to all members (recent articles include "Why Some Insurers Deny Coverage of Cochlear Implants: A Real Life Scenario," "High-Tech Hearing Aids: Are They Right for Your Child?" and "More Than Meets the Ear: Understanding and Optimizing Your Child's Ear molds").

Videotapes

The following are available from the Oberkotter Foundation www. oraldeaf.org or by calling 1-877-ORALDEAF

- *Dreams Spoken Here* (60 minutes) is a detailed exploration of oral deaf education from infancy through adolescence and adulthood, focusing on the critical early years. Includes information on educational techniques and dramatic technological advances in hearing aids and cochlear implants.

- *Dreams Spoken Here* (short version, 20 minutes) is an abridged version of the above film that is usable for those wanting a brief introduction to the issues discussed in the full version of Dreams Spoken Here.

- *Speaking for Myself* (10 minutes) describes how deaf children can learn to speak. Intended for those unfamiliar with oral deaf education.

The following are all available from the League for the Hard of Hearing.

- *Anti-Noise Multi-Media Curriculum Package.* Designed for school use, this multi-media curriculum package is a terrific introduction to the dangers of noise. It includes the videotape *Stop That Noise*, and the audiocassette tape.

- *Assessment of Adult Speechreading Ability.* A tape designed to assist the professional in determining the speechreading ability of hard of hearing and deaf adults. It samples word, sentence and paragraph recognition under three conditions: in quiet without voice; in noise without voice; in noise with voice. Guidelines for interpreting the results are included as are profiles of clients, all with the aim of designing an individualized management program.

- *Don't Forget It!* Depicts the day-to-day problems of an executive with a substantial hearing loss and offers support and solutions to workplace challenges. Hosted by Academy Award–winner Joan Fontaine and produced by MetLife.

- *I Only Hear You When I See Your Face.* An 11-minute video that dramatizes simple accommodations for doctors and nurses to use when communicating with a patient who is hard of hearing or deaf in a hospital setting. Helps improve care and communication, and is particularly very beneficial for sensitivity awareness. Produced by Hope for Hearing Foundation.

- *I See What You're Saying: A Practical Guide to Speechreading.* People who are deaf or hard of hearing and professionals teaching speechreading will find these series of tapes hosted by Gene Wilder a practical tool to enhance visual awareness and improve skills, making real life communication situations easier and more fulfilling. Includes a handbook with suggestions for effective use of the videos.

- *It Happens at Home: A Guide for Language Enrichment for Children Who Are Deaf or Hard of Hearing.* Parents and professionals explore the language enrichment possibilities of daily routines including dressing for the day, cooking lunch, cleaning the kitchen, setting the table, washing dishes and playing outdoors. The video demonstrates reinforcement techniques for parents, family and friends, and explains parental speech styles that facilitate a child's language development.

- *Stop That Noise!* Spencer Christian of Good Morning America fame hosts this video explaining the dangers of excessive noise. Featuring scenes of the usual noisy suspects like city traffic and rock concerts, it also takes a look at the surprising sources of household noise. The tape illustrates warning signs and how the damage occurs as well as pointers on how to protect and conserve hearing. Produced for the League by The Equitable Life Assurance Society of the U.S.

- *The Unfair Hearing Test.* This tape gives listeners the challenging experience of deciphering the English language as if they had a moderate or severe hearing loss, which focuses students on the handbook's activities designed to inspire them to protect their hearing, and to reduce noise in their environment.

- *You & Your Hearing Aid: Sound Advice.* A three-tape orientation program demonstrates the use, maintenance and trouble shooting of hearing aids. (Tape I: *Hearing Loss and Hearing Aids* focuses on how the ear works and examines the variety of hearing aids available. Tape II: *Caring for Your Hearing Aid* deals with the basic care and operation of aids. Tape III: *Hints for People Who Are Hard of Hearing or Deaf and Their Families* examines problems faced by people who have a hearing loss and offers solutions on how to cope with those challenges in an assertive and realistic manner.)

University Programs

Offering oral education training.

- **Eastern Michigan University** is a university-based program offering an undergraduate degree and leading to a B.S. in special education (www.emich.edu).

- **Fontbonne College/St. Joseph's Institute for the Deaf** is a collaboration between Fontbonne College and St. Joseph's Institute for the Deaf offering a four-year undergraduate degree program leading to a bachelor's degree in deaf education. There is also a 14-month master's program in early intervention and deaf education leading to a master of arts degree.

- **Lewis and Clark College/Tucker-Maxon School for the Deaf** is a collaboration between Lewis and Clark College and Tucker Maxon School offering a 14-month program leading to a master's degree in education of children who are deaf and hard of hearing (www.oraldeafed.org/schools/tmos/).

- **Smith College/Clarke School for the Deaf Graduate Teacher Education Program** is a collaboration between Smith College and Clarke School for the Deaf/Center for Oral Education offering a one-year intensive program leading to the master of the education of the deaf degree (www.clarkeschool.org/graduate.html).

- **University of Cincinnati** provides a university-based, two-year program leading to the master of education degree.

- **University of the Incarnate Word/Sunshine Cottage School for the Deaf** is a collaboration between the University of the Incarnate Word and Sunshine Cottage offering a two-year program leading to the master's in education of the hearing impaired (www.sunshinecottage.org).

- **University of Southern California/John Tracy Clinic** is a collaboration between the University of Southern California and the John Tracy Clinic that offers a three-semester program leading to a master's of science in Education. Internet-based distance education program is also available (www.johntracyclinic.org).

- **Washington University/Central Institute for the Deaf** is a collaboration between Washington University and Central Institute for the Deaf offering a two-year program leading to the master of science degree (M.S.) in speech and hearing with a specialization in education of the hearing impaired (www.cid.wustl.edu).

Index